QUEEN OF THE HEAD-HUNTERS

D1353412

Queen of the
of the
Head-hunters

the autobiography of H.H. the Hon.

SYLVIA, LADY BROOKE

The Ranee of Sarawak

SINGAPORE
OXFORD UNIVERSITY PRESS
OXFORD NEW YORK

Oxford University Press

Oxford   New York   Toronto
Delhi   Bombay   Calcutta   Madras   Karachi
Petaling Jaya   Singapore   Hong Kong   Tokyo
Nairobi   Dar es Salaam   Cape Town
Melbourne   Auckland
and associated companies in
Berlin   Ibadan

Oxford is a trade mark of Oxford University Press

First published by Sidgwick & Jackson, London 1970
First issued as an Oxford University Press paperback 1990
Third impression 1991

ISBN 0 19 588960 6

Printed in Malaysia by Peter Chong Printers Sdn. Bhd.
Published by Oxford University Press Pte. Ltd.,
Unit 221, Ubi Avenue 4, Singapore 1440

I dedicate this book to the memory of my husband – the man who was my greatest friend, who never let me down, and who made me laugh more than anyone I have ever known.

S.B.

Tens of thousands yet unborn
Will bless the name of Brooke
  — from the Sarawak National Anthem

§ *Contents*

§ *List of Illustrations*

§ *Preface*

I DO NOT LIKE FACTS, and dates appal me; I'm afraid people who want both will not find much nourishment in the following pages. This is simply the story of my life and of some of the people who have affected it, for better or for worse. And, chiefly, it is about two unusual families, the Bretts and the Brookes, and the part that I played before and after I married the last White Rajah of Sarawak.

I am over eighty now, and memory, I find, is like a will-o'-the-wisp. I can see the light ahead of me and I try to grasp it; it remains elusive, yet the senses are there, the sense of a sound, a touch, a perfume. Smooth oak or cedar wood or silk will bring back an old house or a nursery or a room where love has been born; a perfume recreates the aromatic glory of the jungles of the East. These are the things that linger, that fill one's old age and make one young again.

Some may look upon this book as frivolous, and say that I have skimmed too lightly over the surface of the years; but I have tried to convey a picture, warm and colourful, maybe at times a cruel picture, of the people I have met and the things I have done, and that have been done to me. I don't claim any more for it than that.

I wish to thank my dear friend Frank de Buono for his enthusiasm, his excellent advice and endless patience, without which I should never have been able to compile and complete this book.

SYLVIA BROOKE

Part One

I   *A remote and brilliant father*

I WAS BORN at Number One, Tilney Street, Park Lane, London, on 25 February, 1885.

There was nothing momentous about my arrival into the world. Only my mother's wire-haired terrier, Griz, was violently sick when she first caught sight of me. I was that sort of a baby and she was that kind of a bitch!

I was the last of four bouncing babies, two boys and two girls, only the pity of it was I did not bounce. I was fat and phlegmatic and, from the time I began to think, I became obsessed by the idea that I was never really wanted. My mother had married when she was only seventeen years of age and, having given birth to three children in quick succession, she considered she had had enough, but my father thought otherwise, and my father was never wrong.

My mother was the daughter of Sylvain Van-de-Weyer, who was the founder of the Belgian Monarchy, and the First Minister of King Leopold. Before Louvain was sacked by the Germans the most conspicuous monument in the city was the statue erected to his memory. Later in life Sylvain went to England as Belgian Minister and was the intimate friend of his own king, and of Queen Victoria. He married in England the only daughter of Joshua Bates of Boston, the American partner of the great banking house of Baring.

My father, Reginald Baliol Brett, was descended from William Brett of Brett's Hall in the county of Warwick in the time of Henry III, and on the female side, through the Scotts of Scott's Hall, from the Baliols of Scotland. The eldest son of William Baliol Brett (Master of the Rolls) 1st Viscount Esher, and Eugenie, daughter of Louis Meyer, he was born on 30 June 1852. His younger brother, Eugene, died in the Sudan with General Gordon.

There have never been, as far as I know, any pictures of my father as a child; but I can well imagine he must have been a beautiful little boy with a skin like ivory and roses, calm grey eyes and a soft, curling mouth. He wrote about himself in a book called *Cloud-cap't Towers* which I once possessed, but which has now been borrowed to the point of no return.

'As a child in a poplin frock I had been seated on the lap of a little wizened old man who had once played the violin before Marie Antoinette. Later in my Great Aunt's house in Paris I had been presented to a stout, dark-skinned man with masses of grizzled hair, an enormous hat held curiously between his knees. It was Alexander Dumas.'

The blood of many races flowed within our veins – Scottish, French, American, and Belgian. Somewhere along the line I suspect there had been a little Jewish infiltration and it was rumoured that there had been a connection with Alexander Dumas, perhaps the memory above had something to do with it; which had somewhat shaken the branches of our illustrious family tree.

My father, who had been educated at Eton and Cambridge, was a young man of exquisite tastes, delighting in music, and with a delicate talent for the composition of both poetry and prose. In his early portraits he had the beauty of a young girl and he kept his marvellous skin up to the end. He married at the age of twenty-seven.

I think Reginald Baliol Brett will be remembered as one of the geniuses of his time, not in any particular capacity but as a poet, a musician, a littérateur, a polished diplomat, and a brilliant statesman. He could have filled almost any post, but he preferred

SYLVIA BRETT, AGED SIX

to be free. He began his career as private secretary to Lord Har-
rington when he was twenty-six years of age and remained with
him for almost seven years. He was M.P. for Penryn and Fal-
mouth. He was offered the editorship of the *Daily News* and
refused. He was offered the editorship of the *New Review* and
refused that also. When he was forty-three he became secretary to
H.M. Office of Works and remained there for ten years. He was
asked to write the life of Disraeli, but although amply qualified to
do so, refused. He was asked to become Under-Secretary for the
Colonies; again he refused. Would he be Under-Secretary for
War? No, he would not. What about the Governorship of Cape
Colony? No, he would not do that either. At last he did accept
the post of Honorary Secretary to the Committee for Queen
Victoria's Memorial, and also Lieutenant and Deputy-Governor
of Windsor Castle. He was a member of the Royal Commission
on the South African War, Director of the Opera, and co-editor
of Queen Victoria's letters. He refused the Secretaryship of State
for War, or to become Viceroy of India. He was offered a G.C.B.,
and refused that. Yet this remarkable man was a Commander of
the Legion of Honour and a permanent Member of the Committee of Imperial Defence; Royal Trustee to the British Museum,
Governor of the Imperial College of Science, and Trustee of the
famous Wallace Collection; a Privy Councillor, and Governor of
Windsor Castle. This was the first time the Governor of Windsor
Castle was not a member of the Royal Family. He died on 22
January 1930, having been offered an earldom and refused it.

You can imagine the feeling of having a father as fantastic as
this; it was like being related to the Encyclopaedia Britannica. In
my mother's heart there was no-one greater than Reginald Baliol
Brett, except God. What Reggie said, where Reggie went, how
Reggie felt, were of the utmost importance to her; the very air
she breathed was enchanted by Reggie's rose-tipped cigarettes.
He was the substance and body of her existence, her *raison d'être*.

What incredible children should have been born from such a
union, instead of the disappointing brood my poor little mother
gave birth to!

My sister Dorothy, "Doll", and I were aware at an early age that women were only brought into the world to become the slaves of men. Every morning it was our duty to lace up our brothers' boots, so that even now I can never look at any little boy with that particular footwear without having an intense desire to smack his pugnacious bottom.

We were reared in the very lap of luxury. Butlers, footmen, and maids buzzed around like ornamental but somewhat inefficient flies. I remember they always wore white cotton gloves and I could never make up my mind whether it was they who were supposed to contaminate us, or we them.

We were left very much to ourselves in those early days for our parents were too preoccupied – he with his affairs of State, and she with her wifely adoration. So we quarrelled and fought like a litter of small puppies, and bit and scratched our way through the toddling age into the bewilderments of adolescence.

Children should never be left alone to steep their small souls in doubts and fears and torn emotions. Youth should be such a joyous thing; confident and carefree, without panic or dismay, but it was by no means so with me. I was tormented by imaginative fears. I felt that nobody loved me and that I was the cuckoo in this illustrious family nest. It even seemed to me that my father's voice altered when he spoke to me, as if he were forcing his words through cubes of ice. My mother, my dear possessed mother with her compliant love for Reggie, noticed nothing; her children's emotions were totally unable to break into the absorption of her wifely concern. I spent a great deal of my childhood crying my eyes out in a ten-foot by twelve ivy-papered lavatory at the top of the house.

I think at that time my elder brother, Oliver, had the most charm of us all. He was a good-looking boy with large dark eyes that dreamed. He did not play games, but used to read all day and write poetry. He was a tremendous believer in tradition and ancestors and family trees. I think he was the only one of us who really cared who he was. Maurice was just a plump little boy with rosy cheeks, lamentably spoilt by my father who worshipped him.

This gave him the whip hand over us all. He had black "devil-moods", as we called them, that reduced him to sulky silence, lying face downwards on the floor. These moods distressed my father so much that he would retire into his room: the more deaf Maurice was to reason, the longer my father remained *incommunicado*, with my mother pleading with him outside the door to come out and pacify his son. Yet this perverse little boy grew into a sweet and charming man, without an evil thought in his disposition.

SEX was a forbidden word in the Brett family; for a long time I believed that in order to bring us into the world my mother had laid four gigantic eggs.

We always referred to our parents as "THEY". THEY had this and that. THEY were neglectful and unfair. It was because of THEM that the thought of the future made me shiver in my shoes. It was because of their absorption in one another that they failed to realize we were growing up. It was THEIR fault that a boy of eight, with an enquiring mind, undressed me to see what a little girl was like. As I stood naked and trembling before him he stared at me with his hands in his pockets, whistled, then laughed, and said, "I don't think much of THAT". I did not think much of that either; but I considered it was none of his business to take off my clothes and make a figure of fun of me. I hated him and all boys for ever afterwards. It was THEIR fault that my father's secretary kissed me in the dark, pressing his pale inadequate moustache into my mouth and exploring my twelve-year-old body with his secret searching hands. Thereby was laid the foundation of a wall of horror against all the male sex which took me many years to overcome.

The rich often learn the facts of life as cruelly and clumsily as the poor. These facts can be revealed in a crowded slum or in a dainty drawing-room, but children left too much alone at the most vulnerable moments of their lives can discover only as best they can the difference between love and lust, frigidity and fire.

Our homes both in London and at Winkfield, Windsor Forest, were very beautiful. "Orchard Lea" was filled with old oak, cedar wood, and tapestried walls. The garden had been transformed from a wilderness of forest trees and tangled undergrowth by Princess Louise, Duchess of Argyle, into a bower of roses and red brick paths with wrought-iron gates. Across the road lay Windsor Great Forest.

But "Orchard Lea" was too large for four lonely children to run wild in. We feared the vastness of those shadowy rooms, with the jewelled rapiers which my father collected, glistening from the dark walls. There were winding passages which I would run down with my heart thumping against my ribs. On and on they seemed to go into eternity, before, at last, I reached the narrow corkscrew staircase that led to my attic room. The timbers would creak from the hall below and the shadows of the rapier handles would show up like gallows against the ill-lit walls. I imagined there were hands stretched out to catch me, cruel diamond eyes probing through the darkness – all the terrors of a lonely and imaginative child.

2 *Princes to tea*

W<small>E LIVED</small> for long spells at "Orchard Lea", but they seem now to be a collection of vague visions of famous people flashing on to the screen and then gone. Lord Rosebery, Sir William Harcourt, Arthur Balfour and his brother Gerald, Sir John Morley – a kaleidoscope of fame passing almost unheeded before our inexperienced eyes. I do well remember Lord Rosebery learning to ride a bicycle in our garden, a most unusual performance for any member of the aristocracy to indulge in in those far-off days. We would all turn out to watch, with awe and admiration, as the great man swayed uncertainly in the saddle. He would flash past us, his noble features contorted with fear and his eyes starting out of his head. The trouble was that once mounted, he had not the slightest idea how to get off. Around and around the garden he pedalled until we would hear a resounding crash, and my father would rush to the nearest rose bush and drag him from amongst the thorns.

There are people one may meet perhaps only once during a lifetime and yet the memory of them remains more vivid than that of some friend one has known for many years. The Emperor of Germany was such a memory and such a man. I only met him for a fleeting moment, yet even today I can visualize the intense alertness of his face and hear his strange guttural accent.

My sister and her governess had heard that he was out shooting in Windsor Park with the Prince of Wales – later King George V – so we bicycled there from "Orchard Lea" and followed the pheasant drive as closely as we could. The Kaiser was in an extremely jocular mood for he knew how excellent a shot the Prince of Wales was, and he, with his one arm, was even better. He was dressed in light blue with a Tyrolean hat with a black feather in it. He had four men, also dressed in blue, with four guns. Each gun was handed to him at full cock because he could only shoot with one arm, the other being short and withered. He killed one hundred and seventy-eight pheasants and three hundred and thirty rabbits during that day.

When the shoot was over, and the birds and rabbits lay out on the grass, someone in the Prince of Wales's entourage recognized us. We were dragged forward to be presented, two hot, dishevelled, dumb little girls. The Kaiser was a great friend of my father's at that time and was interested to see what his daughters were like. He bombarded us with questions for which, thank God, he never waited for answers. I remember standing first on one leg and then on the other, completely mesmerized by his disturbing personality. His eyes were wild and bulging and he gave the impression of vivid unrepose. He shaped his words like a dog barking at a distant foe. He made the unimportant and trivial remarks any man might make to two awkward and goggling little girls, but, we felt the force of his fierce energy.

The only two young people who ever came frequently to "Orchard Lea" at that time were Wilfred Sheridan and Teddy Seymour. Wilfred was a descendant of Richard Brinsley Sheridan; he had no use for any of us. Teddy, on the other hand, would stay with us for months at a time; my father adored him; and although he was only eighteen, he was not in the least afraid of my father and would tease him to his heart's content. He would say to my mother "Let's rag Reggie today", and the rows and arguments they had could be heard all over the house. He was extremely good-looking, with his golden hair, bright blue eyes, and laughing voice. I used to fetch and carry for him like a spaniel;

my family called me "Teddy's shadow", and Doll and my two brothers jeered at me for my devotion. But he was charming to me in his good-natured lordly way, and was the only person who at that time threw me a few crumbs of consolation.

The two people I really passionately loved when I was about six or seven were W. T. Stead, who was drowned in the *Titanic*, and my grandfather, Viscount Esher, Master of the Rolls. I suppose if I had realized what a great man he was, one of the finest judges of his time, I would have been awe-struck, but to me he was just the most darling and lovable old man, and, above all, he was devoted to me. I remember how I would sit on his knee, stroking the snow-white hair that grew like a soft halo around his head, and implore him to marry me. "I'll never marry anyone else," I would assure him. He would chuckle and say "What about your grandmother? Don't you think we had better ask her first?" But I was afraid of my grandmother and told him that this was to be a secret between him and me.

Once he took me into his court with him and I sat in an enormous chair with great carved arms. I was wearing a green velvet frock with a lace collar and black button boots. The prisoner being tried was very poor, a white-faced shrew of a man with hands like claws that clung to the rail in front of him. I remember he was given a very light sentence, and as he was swept from the dock, like a leaf in a gust of wind, I heard my grandfather mutter, "Poor devil, I would have so liked to let him off."

I realize now that "Orchard Lea" was one of the loveliest places in the world, and the garden was just the kind that every country house in England should possess. On the lawn there was an enormous weeping-willow that looked like Queen Victoria in a crinoline; and, right at the end, what my parents called "Pan's Garden". Here, amidst a riot of flowers and green grass paths, there was an immense statue of Pan playing his pipes, his shoulders bent and his face grinning with evil. This so terrified me that I would never venture there alone. A red-brick terrace ran down one side of the garden, and beyond the terrace was a meadow where my father used to keep his race horses. In the kitchen garden there were herbaceous borders, brick paths, and a high brick wall upon which grew great golden plums. Behind the borders, netted fruits – strawberries, raspberries, and red currants – were artfully concealed; and beyond this was a little orchard where we all had our own apple trees. My tree was stunted and ugly, but I loved it and called it "Rosy" because of the shining red apples that grew in profusion on its branches.

There was a wood at "Orchard Lea", and here we built wig-wams of twigs, foliage, bits of old sacking and cloth stolen from the ash-can in our back yard, and would play at being wild Indians with their squaws. I was always Maurice's squaw and was often kept in the wigwam all afternoon because he said I was too ugly to come out. Doll was my elder brother's squaw. She was allowed to roam wherever she wanted, because Oliver could find no means of keeping her in. No-one could ever make Doll do anything she did not want to. She was never afraid of her brothers as I was. I feared and disliked them, but was forced to be in all their games. When the time came for them to go to school I used to pray to God that they would never come back.

Living as close as we did to Windsor Castle, it was only natural that we should see a great deal of the Royal Family, both in our own house and at Windsor. When Prince Edward (now Duke of Windsor) was about eight years old, he would come over to "Orchard Lea" with Prince Albert and Princess Mary, and their tutor. The Princes would wear little white sailor suits and Princess Mary a very short, very tightly pleated skirt.

During the course of one afternoon Prince Edward and Princess Mary disappeared, and we were left alone with Prince Albert. We did not dare tell our parents or the tutor, but rushed hither and thither searching and calling their names. Only Prince Albert was completely undisturbed. "They will turn up all right," he stammered confidently, "they always do."

After half-an-hour of agonizing doubt, they returned, red in the face and looking guilty, but they refused to tell us where they had been. All the time we were playing Prince Edward seemed inattentive and listless. Suddenly my father appeared in a furious temper. A message had been sent from the house opposite to the effect that all the baby ducks had been killed and were laid out in a row beside the lake. Was there anyone who knew anything about THAT?

"I do," replied Prince Edward, "because it was I who did it."

"I was there too," said Princess Mary.

"She wasn't really there," protested Prince Edward, "she just came with me, that's all."

My father could not have been more annoyed. He told Prince Edward that he was to go across to the house at once and apologize to the owner, whose name was Mrs Cochrane. At first Prince Edward refused, standing stubbornly with his legs apart and his hands deep in his pockets, but eight-year-old defiance met with failure, and soon he was on his way. I remember Mrs Cochrane saying afterwards that the apology was of such sweetness and charm that she found it impossible to resent the loss of her ducklings.

There was another incident one afternoon when all three children disappeared. The hubbub that ensued was unbelievable. The royal tutor glared at us as potential murderers and my father and mother rushed wildly about the garden calling, "David, Mary, Albert!"

"Perhaps they've gone out in the road and got run over," suggested my sister helpfully.

The tutor's face was a study. He went pink and then white and then a kind of ethereal green. He kept repeating "Oh dear, oh dear, this is a calamity!", and blowing his nose on an enormous white silk handkerchief. Then a piercing scream came from the stables and shouts of "Whoa there! Steady now!" Then the sharp crack of a whip. Round to the stables we tore, hot, dishevelled, and terrified; and before our eyes was the most amazing picture. The Royal children had managed to drag our big wagonette into the yard. Perched upon the driver's seat was Prince Edward holding the reins and cracking a long whip. Harnessed into the shafts were Princess Mary and Prince Albert, prancing, kicking, and neighing as loudly as they could. My father shouted to Prince

Edward to get down at once, but the little boy laughed and shook his head. The tutor, I remember, clambered up on to the wagonette and grabbed Prince Edward unceremoniously from his seat and smacked his bottom, whilst my father and mother struggled to unharness the kicking, neighing "horses". The Royal children were taken back to Windsor Castle very early that day, and it was a long time before they visited us again.

My father used to say that Prince Edward had the eyes of an angel and a special "look" on his small face that might make him one of the greatest kings in history. In a fervour of desire to make myself noticed I endeavoured to cultivate that same expression. I gazed into space as if in rapt contemplation of some celestial being, but my father's voice broke in upon this mighty reverie, "Sylvia looks constipated, we had better give her a dose." That was the end of my soulful impersonation of the future heir to the throne!

Our parents arranged that my sister and I should have dancing classes at Windsor Castle with the little Battenbergs, the children of Princess Beatrice, youngest daughter of Queen Victoria. These classes were under the supervision of Queen Victoria herself, and the instructress was Mrs Wordsworth, who, it was whispered, possessed a wooden leg. Queen Victoria would sit in a great armchair, which seemed to us like a throne; then this petrifying, rotund little matriarch, with her dusty crinoline and her white hair drawn into a white cap, would thump with her stick on the floor while Mrs Wordsworth roared out her commands with the voice of an infuriated sergeant-major.

When I was about seven years old I had really nicely shaped legs, and Queen Victoria would make me stand in front of the class – much to my embarrassment, the fury of my sister, and the derision of the little Princesses.

3 *Innocence and death*

NOBODY who was not SOMEBODY meant a thing to my father. It was not so much that he was a snob as that he enjoyed Royalty and titles, and was genuinely and shamelessly impressed with Earls and Dukes and Duchesses, who paraded through his spacious rooms and elegant gardens, while my mother paid homage to the great whom "her Reggie" had invited there. I thought her self-effacement was weak and foolish in those days. Now, when I look back at the memory of them and their fifty years and more of perfect human harmony, I realize that two such brilliant stars could not have shone in the same house without the ultimate destruction of them both. So she stood meekly in the shadow of his glory and let her personality pale and fade against his. She was, I think, almost as clever and colourful as he was, but she dimmed her light to strengthen his because he was the god at whose shrine she humbly worshipped. They were never really happy when away from one another and unless she went with him to London he felt lost, like an actor without an audience. Then, when they returned to "Orchard Lea" there was my brother Maurice who was always very close to my father. Sometimes I could see jealousy rise like a flash in my mother's large dark eyes and she would say something sarcastic to her beloved Reggie that she would afterwards regret.

At every meal Doll and I would sit speechless. What could we possibly say that would interest these two brilliant people? But our silence would irritate my father. He could not and would not tolerate stupidity. He would never talk down to any of us, though he must have known that we had not the slightest idea of what he was saying – the maxims of Napoleon, Mary Queen of Scots and her infatuation for Bothwell, Caesar, religion, philosophy. . . . Only my mother could keep up with him. I think he must have had an intuition when he first met that slim shy girl of sixteen that she was the only one who could reach the standard of his intellect.

When I was told that my grandfather was dead and that he had sent his blessing to my brothers, but never a word to my sister or myself, I was heartbroken. He was buried at Esher; but only my two brothers were allowed to attend the funeral. And, reinforcing the bitterness I felt, my father simply ignored my existence. I remember him saying to Maurice, "Continue with your usual life. It is what your grandfather would have wished, and what I would wish were I in his place. Death has no terrors."

"No," I thought, as I went weeping to my room, "it's life that holds all the fears." The future seemed to hold no hope for me.

I do not remember when it was that I made up my mind that my life was not worth living. First I tried ptomaine poisoning. I bought a tin of sardines from the village shop, opened it and put it on top of my cupboard for seven days. There is no need to describe what the contents of that tin were like by then: I forced myself to swallow them, and washed them down my throat with a glass of water. I then brushed my hair, put on my prettiest nightgown, asked God to forgive me and went quietly to bed.

The next morning I woke up normally. I suffered no nausea, no vomiting, no muscular cramp, no prostration. I actually felt better than before!

My next attempt was pneumonia. It was mid-winter, one of those rare English winters when drifts of snow settle on the rooftops and weigh down the trees. There was a high turret just outside my bedroom window with plenty of room on it, where I would sit in the summer and read. I waited until I thought everyone would be asleep; then I crawled from my window and lay naked in the snow. At first the agony of my warm body sinking into that icy softness was almost more than I could bear, but after a while I was lulled into a drowsy contentment. The stars became blurred, weird shapes passed over the moon. I remember thinking, "Now I am dying, will anyone care?" Then my nurse's angry voice shouting, "In God's mercy, child, whatever are you trying to do?" Her arms dragged me roughly back into my room. The next morning there was not even a sneeze. My two attempts at suicide had failed.

Strange how the most intense moments of one's life may seem trivial and of little consequence to the outside world. Here was I, a girl barely twelve years old, endeavouring to destroy herself. Against all my religious beliefs, my dreams, and my desires, I was deliberately slamming the door in the face of any future that God might hold in store for me. Folly of youth and the workings of self-pity! When I think of it now, I shudder at the thought of what I would have missed, just because my father ignored and neglected me, or my mother had failed to kiss me before I went to bed.

We grew up with a mixture of confused ideas surrounding us. Royalty, politicians, priests, artists, and musicians filled our adolescent lives. We were never allowed to meet children of our own age for fear of mental contamination. If we were not exactly ornamental, my sister and I, at least we were pure.

I became more and more obsessed by the longing to be loved, for the tender attention of my preoccupied parents. There was so much love inside me and I had no-one upon whom to lavish it. I could not believe that in the vast world there was not one human being who would worship me.

I spent day after day reading in my little attic room, immersing myself in the vivid worlds of Emile Zola, Guy de Maupassant, and Edgar Allan Poe. If anything, they deepened my impression of mankind's hatred and fear of itself. Zola's description of the birth of a child, de Maupassant's "Yvette", and Edgar Allan Poe's tales of horror in *The Murders in the Rue Morgue*, filled me with unhappiness and dread, yet I could not put them away on the shelf and forget them. Their very ugliness fitted my mood; I trembled to think of them and yet I could think of nothing else. I was proud that I was different from my brothers and sister, who went out into the garden and played with natural and normal things. I wondered what they would have thought if I had told them of my father's secretary, with his exploring hands, and of the bored, inquisitive boy who had torn off my clothes. Was that really all there was to look forward to, this groping and fumbling and wanting?

My brothers and sister had little use for me in those early years. They tormented me as children will torment some small animal unable to protect itself, and my excessive timidity only encouraged them. My homely, brooding face displeased my parents; I was a misfit in their elegant surroundings. "The Ugly Duckling" is a phrase used by too many careless tongues: its wounds may last a lifetime.

I often think back on the years of waste and loss during my childhood when I was consumed with jealousy and envy of my sister's golden hair, my eldest brother's dark good looks and the petting of the little boy who was my father's favourite son. I seemed to be the runt of a litter of pedigree puppies, snapping and biting with senseless fury at the red-cheeked and dull little brother who so charmed my father. What had he got, I asked myself, as I snuffled and wept in the ivy-papered lavatory; and I have never found the answer. What bond of adoration linked my brilliant father and his stolid son?

4 *The marriage market*

NEXT, from those years of my youth comes a vague vision of masses of flowers, Chopin's funeral march, and Queen Victoria's coffin being drawn upon a gun carriage in front of a solemn procession of Kings, Queens, Princes, and Princesses. Then King Edward's Coronation; a sick man standing bravely to be crowned. I remember my father exhausted and frantic with worry, as if the whole of the British Empire rested on his shoulders.

It is amazing how, when you get old, you return again and again, not to the friends that you knew so well, but to the spectacular strangers that passed before your green and credulous eyes. The Emperor of Germany, King Edward VII with his truly beautiful Queen; George V when he was still Prince of Wales, and afterwards when he became King. A parade of Royalty that my father so delighted in, lodged in my memory, unrelated to historical facts; just colourful figures in a tapestry of time.

My early days of adolescence were darkened by the Boer War and the fact that my beloved Teddy Seymour was sent abroad. He was wounded in the foot and returned to "Orchard Lea" hobbling, with a stick, and wearing an enormous carpet slipper that we nicknamed "Kruger".

The Relief of Mafeking! What a night that was! The songs, and Kipling's "Absent-minded Beggar" recited from every stage.

I remember collecting pictures of all the famous soldiers who had taken part in the war. Kitchener, French, Baden-Powell, Methuen, Sir George White, and Redvers Buller. I never imagined then that years later one of these men would become one of my greatest friends.

The time had now come for my sister Doll to be presented at Court. She had a soft delicate face like my father's, and her high-piled hair had turned from gold to a deep auburn. Outwardly she was intensely feminine, but it soon became apparent that this elegant façade concealed a masculine independence of spirit. She scorned the ritual of match-making, snubbed her escorts, and as soon as the round of parties was over, cut off her hair, dressed like a boy, and became one of the best-known figures in the painters' pubs of Chelsea. She learned to draw at the Slade School of Art, and eventually she packed up her belongings and went off to Taos, New Mexico with D. H. Lawrence. There she became one of the finest painters of Red Indian portraits and of pictures of their famous fire-dance.

It then became my turn to be flung into the vortex of London Society, and my poor mother took endless trouble collecting the frocks I should wear. She had so hoped that Doll would have been swept from the debutante shelves as soon as she appeared. I do not think she had any such illusions about me.

I look back on that wonderful first season of mine, with the doors of Londonderry House, Devonshire House, Apsley House, and Stafford House flung wide open, and I know that I lived through the most glamorous and glittering finale of England's fame. Ancient names, historic associations, the cream of London's Society, all paraded before my wide-open eyes; marquises, noblemen and their ladies, of a time when titles really meant something, and were not bargained for and bought by the highest bidder.

To have witnessed the Royal Quadrille and seen King Edward VII lead his Queen on to the dance floor, Gottlieb's famous orchestra filling the dazzling ballroom of Buckingham Palace with a perfection of splendour and grace – those were the nights of elegance and poise. To have heard Melba and Caruso in *La Bohême*, Kirby Lunn and Adelina Patti; Richter conducting the huge orchestra as it thundered through Wagner; to have known Enrico Caruso, that moody, mischief-making, happy-go-lucky, child of Naples; all these have left me something melodious to remember all my life. I was there at Covent Garden the evening his mighty voice was silenced for ever; when he suddenly failed on his famous high note and not a sound came from that poor sick throat of his. He stood there with the tears pouring down his face as the heavy curtain slowly dropped in front of him, and we knew we would never hear his like again.

We went to dinner parties, my mother and I; to garden parties, concerts, race meetings, and formidable "At Homes". We flogged that Season relentlessly, but at the end of it all, it had to be admitted that as a debutante I was a flop.

But my parents were determined that, somehow, I should be chosen. Day after day we lunched at the Savoy Grill, and "Lord Esher's table" became the rendezvous of military men, authors, Members of Parliament, and editors of every famous newspaper. It was there I met for the first time Sir John French, who afterwards became the Earl of Ypres and one of my very dearest friends. I met J. M. Barrie and Bernard Shaw, Beerbohm Tree, Marie Tempest, and Ivor Novello whose charm and beauty endeared him to everyone he spoke to. Being presented to so many famous people made me become more aware of my personal appearance. I bought a little black velvet jacket and a black straw hat with a rose nodding on the front of it; secretly I purchased a pair of pin curls and thrust them on either side of my face, softening somewhat my puritanical appearance, until one day they blew from my head and I could not afford to replace them.

Yet no matter how much I yearned to get married, the fear of men had grown up with me. Strange how incidents that have hurt remain for ever walled up within us; a disparaging remark, a callous laugh; a trust betrayed or a trust forsworn.

What strange fascination was it that drew me towards my father, with his vague neglect of my existence, and then, that sudden sadistic awareness that he could tease me to tears by asking me questions he knew I could not answer? Why must I go on trying to prove to him that of all his offspring I was the noblest and the best? Was it only jealousy of my brother or rage that I could not express myself without stumbling and stuttering and dissolving into tears? I do not know, but even now when I think of my brilliant father there is an ache in my heart because I missed my share of him.

I remember hearing of a bomb that exploded on the doorstep of No. 2, Tilney Street. My mother had returned alone from the theatre and must have stepped over it as she entered the house. She was standing by a table eating some grapes when the door blew right past her. It was a French bomb, full of melanite, French newspaper scraps and French screws. Nobody ever discovered why it had been placed there, but it was believed that it had been meant for a famous judge who lived next door as revenge for some criminal he had sentenced.

Then suddenly it seemed that I had found my real refuge. A magazine called *The Woman at Home* advertised a prize of twenty pounds for a love story of 4,000 words. I made up my mind to enter the competition. Four thousand words was a lot of writing about a subject on which I knew so little, but as I began, inspiration came to me. I would make my hero a stammering demigod, then every word he uttered would become two or three! I called my story "Sweet William", and it positively oozed with sentimental ardour.

Lo and behold, my masterpiece won the twenty pounds! It was not so much the fact that I had won the money, as the fact that I had achieved something, that made me happy. Each word I wrote was like a lighted candle in the darkness of my little attic room.

It was after this that J. M. Barrie and Bernard Shaw adopted me as their literary godchild; and I settled down to be an authoress. Each story I wrote lifted a burden from me, as if I had shed a weight of words that had been consuming me. I wanted through my pen to be able to strike back at the world I believed had always borne a grudge against me. I wanted to hurt somebody as I felt that I myself had been hurt by my family's lack of appreciation. Magazines were filled with my effusions as I began to learn the market value of words. I was on the first rung of the ladder – but I fancied myself right at the top.

I sent a collection of my work to J. M. Barrie, in the form of a book I proposed to entitle *Pan and the Little Green Gate*. The stories were hardly more than the chatterings of a child; nevertheless my dear literary godfather wrote back approving of them and offering to show them to Hodder & Stoughton. "I am tremendously glad that I like them so much", he ended up, "Yours always, J. M. Barrie".

You can imagine the effect this letter had upon my already grand conception of myself, how it inflated my ego and puffed me up with pride. I flourished it in front of my father; I read and re-read it before my sister's eyes: J. M. Barrie liked my stories and was going to see that they were published.

It seemed that the sorrows of the world lay in those deep-set eyes of his, yet no-one knew better than he did which way he was going. I remember once saying something to him about stupid people, and how he turned to me and replied "Don't despise stupid people. They are often so much better than the clever, and it is so ordinary to be merely clever and smart these days. Every other man you meet is clever." But he could also be quiet and unapproachable, and sometimes I would spend a whole day with him, neither of us saying a word; yet these silences of his were not in any way embarrassing. He would sit and chew on his pipe, curled up in a chair. I would sit opposite him, watching that small bird-like face and those brooding eyes, thinking what a contrast he was to my other literary godfather, George Bernard Shaw.

G. B. S. made mental love to all women in his fantastic letters; exciting and stimulating, he could have swept any woman off her feet, had she really believed the things he wrote to her. But George Bernard Shaw was in love only with himself. Soft Irish words whispered easily from his mouth as if his whole lean frame vibrated with their music, with never an awkward sentence or a misplaced phrase as he swayed back and forth with his hands thrust deep in his pockets. Tongue in cheek, he laughed at the world, and above all he was able to laugh at himself. He was as voluble and conscious of his glory as J. M. Barrie was silently aware of his.

The latter's interest in my stories worked wonders, and *Pan and the Little Green Gate* was accepted for publication. I do not know what has become of this first book of mine, which was dedicated to J. M. Barrie. It turned into one of those volumes that pass from hand to hand and vanish, but I still have some of the newspaper cuttings and criticisms pasted into a book. They said my stories had delicacy and charm; they were touching and poetic, and at the same time displayed considerable knowledge of human life. One paper, the most flattering of all, said, "Open the book and walk at once into the magic atmosphere of fairyland. *Pan and the Little Green Gate* is one of the best written, quaintest and most fascinating volumes of stories that has appeared in recent years."

This encouragement inspired me to go on writing. I linked together a collection of stories all set in one street, and sent my readers prying into every house, uncovering the lives there. One of them was No. 2, Tilney Street, next door to where I had been born, and I called this book *The Street with the Seven Houses*. It was received with unanimous applause. "Not for a long while", the *Pall Mall* announced, "has a volume of short sketches appealed to us more than this. . . . With wider experience, Miss Brett will write a story that will put her into great prominence."

This was over sixty years ago, and I have not yet written that prominent and famous book.

One of the short stories was about my sister and myself and I called it "The Left Ladies". Bernard Shaw had a few things to say about it and wrote me the following letter:

Honourable Sylvia:
    Yes, this is a serious matter being a 'Left Lady', but I don't think it is the plainness. If I was an attractively tattooed South Sea

islander of an age at which one can engage in some adventures without becoming ridiculous and I met you under a palm tree, I should have no hesitation (apart from shyness) than I should about eating an exceptionally delicious plum with all the bloom on – but all these unfortunate companions and associates of yours, the title, the Windsor Castle and the Royal pals and all the rest of it, make you so frightfully expensive and terrifying that the nobs can't afford it and the snobs daren't. Something must be done. The simplest way is to select your man and ask him. It's quite usual, they always used to ask me! Or why not advertise? "Wanted by an old maid of twenty who can give exceptional references (photograph if stamps enclosed) a young man to keep company. One desirous of improving his social position preferred. Special opportunities. Must not be literary, as one writer in the family is enough. Apply Sylvia (real name and looks it) c/o George V, Windsor Castle."

Ever yours,

G.B.S.

That such men as Shaw and Barrie appreciated my work most surely meant that I was on the ladder to the stars. I could already see myself in the bookcase of perpetual fame. I remembered that Bernard Shaw had said, "Select your man and ask him!" I made up my mind that that was exactly what I would do. Why I selected J. M. Barrie to be my man, God only knows, but it seemed to me that after his broken marriage he was even more isolated than I was. I actually made myself believe that it was me he needed, and I sat down and wrote him a letter asking him to marry me.

I blush even now when I recall this letter of proposal, the outpourings of a clumsy frustrated debutante to this melancholy little man, but at the time I felt no shame in asking him to marry me; it was all part of the fantasy of our friendship. His letter of refusal was typical of him; I could almost see the half-smile on his small brooding face as he wrote, "I am flattered and honoured but don't you think we are better as we are?" Then he told me that because of my love for children I was the "Wendy" of his "Peter Pan".

"One day you will marry, dear Sylvia," he wrote, "and bear a tremendous family of your own." I did not believe him, but it lifted my heart and healed the wound of his refusal.

It was not very long after this that, quietly and unknowingly, I took the road that led me after seven tempestuous years into my Paradise.

5   *Letter from a Ranee*

CALL IT FATE, that caused a letter to be sent to my mother from someone who lived four miles from our home, but whom she had never even seen. The writer explained that she was forming a small amateur orchestra in which she was very anxious my sister and I should join. It was signed MARGARET, RANEE OF SARAWAK.

As my mother and father perused this letter my whole future, had I known it, hung balanced between their hands. They did not really approve of our joining the orchestra. It seemed unconventional, and the picturesque title of the inaugurator annoyed my father, but for the first time my mother's voice prevailed. She thought it would do us good, she said, and it most certainly could not do us any harm.

My sister and I scampered to our rooms and tore down every book of reference we could find, seated there by the fire, Doll read me the story of the first White Rajah.

James Brooke was born in the European suburb of Benares called Secrore, on 29 April 1803. He was the second son and favourite child of one Thomas Brooke, handsome and headstrong, and his parents doted on him. At the age of sixteen he obtained an Ensign's commission in the 6th Madras Infantry, and later he fought and was badly wounded in the First Burmese War. He returned to his family at Combe Grove, Bath, an invalid; so he sent in his resignation, and went on a voyage to China. It was then that he saw for the first time the islands of the Asiatic archipelago. To James Brooke they seemed an open invitation to adventure. With his father's help, he bought the brig *Findlay* in partnership with a certain Captain Kennedy. But James Brooke had not been brought into the world to be a trader; he was the kind that kings are made of, and somewhere there was a country waiting for him to rule.

In 1833 Thomas Brooke died, leaving £30,000 to his son, and James purchased a vessel of his own, the *Royalist*, the famous schooner of one hundred and forty tons that was to be the first British yacht to dip her inquisitive forefoot into Sarawak waters.

It was while he was in Singapore that James Brooke first heard of rebellion in Borneo. The ruler, a Malay prince named Raja Muda Hassim, was desperate, and incapable of restoring law and order. All that was known about Borneo at that time was that it was infested by Dyak head-hunters, and by pirates who roamed the coast, destroying native trade and terrifying the people. To James Brooke it seemed a heaven-sent opportunity. "God has made me", he said, "to be the suppressor of head-hunting and slavery in Sarawak."

So in 1840, with a handful of Englishmen, a few native boatmen and little else but his cutlass and one muzzle-loading gun, James Brooke landed in Kuching. He told Raja Muda Hassim that he was confident he could put down the rebellion; but only on condition that he was made sole leader in place of the unscrupulous Governor, Pangaran Makota. Raja Muda Hassim confessed that he was afraid of Makota, and dared not put this Englishman in his place. "Very well," replied Brooke, "as you have chosen against me there is no need for me to remain amongst you."

In an agony of doubt and fear, Raja Muda Hassim at last reached a decision, and made his famous declaration:

"If only you will remain," he cried, "I will give you all my country. I will give you my government and my trade. All these things you can have, and your generation after you, if only you will not desert me in my hour of need!"

This was enough for James Brooke. With his tiny force he suppressed the rebellion, and returned in triumph to Kuching, where he was received with acclamation and treated as a god. A year later, on 24 September 1841, Raja Muda Hassim fulfilled his promise and proclaimed James Brooke, then thirty-eight years old, the first White Rajah of Sarawak.

So began the unique personal rule of the Brooke family in Borneo, which James maintained until his death in 1868, and handed on to his nephew, Charles.

It was from the wife of Charles Brooke, the second White Rajah, then living apart from her husband at Ascot, that my mother had received the letter.

When my sister stopped reading, we sat and stared at one another. We had been quite carried away by the intensely romantic tale of pirates and head-hunters and a man who had been made a king. Moreover, it was true. The Ranee Margaret of Sarawak was fact, not fiction; and we were going to meet her.

I shall never forget our entry into Grey Friars. The Ranee Margaret was seated regally in a high-backed chair, talking about herself and her three sons. There was nothing very feminine about her either in her manner or in the way she decorated her ordinary and almost ugly home; but she could dominate a room with her personality and her magnetic eyes, and enchant everyone in it.

Everyone, that is, except my father, who loathed her. How much was genuine about her, beyond her music and her love for her sons, was hard to say; and we did not speculate. She flattered and petted us; we were as enchanted as the rest; and the bleak little music room, with its book-lined walls and dreary cretonnes, became our sanctuary. The week held only one day for us – the day we pedalled our way to South Ascot. In the hall of her house there was a huge macaw with scarlet wings, a terrifying bird, which was tied by a chain to a stand. When this strange woman was not seated at her piano she would recline in a blue armchair with the green parrot perched upon her wrist.

My sister played the side drums and kettle drum extremely well. I had no special talent, and with some apprehension chose the big drum, cymbals, and triangle. No sooner had we joined the Grey Friars orchestra than we began to rehearse for a charity performance of "His Excellency, the Governor", with the Ranee's youngest son in the star part. Harry Brooke, or the "Tuan Bungsu" as he was known in Sarawak, was a wonderful amateur actor and might well have become a professional but for the shyness that seemed to be inborn in all the Ranee's sons.

When the rehearsal was over, the Ranee Margaret would ask my sister and myself to tea and then she would often talk about her life in Sarawak. She was estranged from her husband but had lived many years with him in the country he ruled on the northwest coast of Borneo. She had had three children, two boys and a girl, but they had died in their infancy of cholera and had been buried at sea. Because of the need for a son and heir, she had returned to the cold indifferent man she did not love and had borne him three more sons.

She had had isolated moments of pleasure amongst the Dyaks and Malays which had displeased her husband and made him envy her. Their marriage had ended when he destroyed her pet doves and served them in a pie for her supper. We listened spell-bound to her stories; and I can see my sister, Doll, her great dark eyes fixed on the Ranee's face like a girl in love.

It was not until the Ranee's eldest son came home on leave from Sarawak that her scheme began to be revealed. Here were three shy, unapproachable, unmarried men who refused to go out anywhere or see anyone: and an inheritance which made it essential for them to marry. Only a clever woman could have found the solution to this problem in an orchestra composed entirely of desperate and willing virgins, duly assembled twice a week for her sons to look over. Blondes and brunettes, all shapes and sizes, nice, healthy, simple, unsullied, unspoiled girls. Not notably ornamental: in fact, a more homely group could hardly be imagined: and yet, in the fullness of time, each one of her sons became engaged to a girl in the Grey Friars orchestra.

You could not have found three more charming men than Vyner, Bertram, and Harry Brooke. Harry, the youngest, had his mother's charm and easy warmth of manner. Bertram, or "Adeh" as he was called, was a little diffident and constrained and covered with confusion when addressed. He had almost foreign manners, a reflection of his younger days in Heidelberg. Vyner was extremely handsome, with smooth fair skin tanned a rich brown by the tropical sun. He had the fine Brooke nose that nature has perpetuated in the outline of the Matang mountain in Sarawak; but he was so shy you felt that if you turned and spoke to him, he would rush headlong from the room.

I cannot remember when I first became aware of Vyner Brooke, of those startling blue eyes watching me across the room. I was too busy with my deafening drum and clashing cymbals. But, one day, he drew up a chair and sat beside me. I heard his quiet voice say, "I want you to let me tune your drum for you. May I, Miss Sylvia?" Nineteen hostile faces glared at me and nineteen disappointed hearts wished I would drop dead.

I wished then that my pin curls had not blown away. I wished too that there were buttons in my sleeve cuffs instead of safety pins. I was desperately aware of my dumbness and the dull fixity of my expression. It hardly occurred to me that because a man had offered to tune my drum for me, he was beginning to offer me his heart.

6   *Letter from a Ranee's son*

AY AFTER DAY we pedalled up the pine-tree drive, past St Anthony, and through the door which led us to such happiness. When we went home we sat at meals like two stricken souls from another world and occasionally gave one another sly secret looks that incensed my already infuriated parents. They knew that my sister was enraptured with the Ranee Margaret; what they did not know was that she had three sons whom she was determined to marry off. They did not know this until the orchestra folded for a while and I received a letter from Vyner Brooke. I shall never forget the stir it caused. My letters were so few and far between, my correspondence limited to J. M. Barrie and Bernard Shaw, that this little grey envelope with legible but scrawling writing landed like a bomb in our midst:

My dear Sylvia,

I hope you will pardon the liberty I take in writing to you but I have in my possession your drumstick, which you left hidden in the innermost recess of the carriage on that last Saturday night. I have kept it as a memento of the band, but will give it up on the occasion of your next visit here. This will be safer than sending it by post. I go to Gloucester tomorrow for a few days and if you care to write my address is Chesterton House, Cirencester.

Yours sincerely,

Vyner Brooke

P S. Are you writing any more stories?

The letter was handed round the table, held by the tips of disapproving fingers, and read and re-read as if to find some hidden motive there. No comment was made, no objection raised at the time. How could there be when this man was only informing me that he had found my drumstick? I wrote and told him of course he could keep the drumstick and that I hoped I would see him on Wednesday at the theatre in Windsor. Sure enough, he was there, but I was strictly kept away from him and when the play was over I was swept out of the theatre before I could even look round to see where he was.

The next thing I heard was that Adeh was engaged to Gladys Palmer of the Huntley & Palmer biscuit family. She had played the mandoline in the Grey Friars orchestra. I received another letter from Vyner of which my parents strongly disapproved. It was a harmless, simple letter but it revealed the fact that I had been secretly writing to him. He thanked me for the stories I had sent him and for telling him that he could keep the drumstick. He signed it, "Yours sincerely, Vyner Brooke" and addressed it to "The Second Drummer of the G.F.O.S." His letter seemed to me discretion itself. I could not see that he was in any way culpable of duplicity or deceit. My parents and my sister Doll led me to believe that there was "something in it". They said they could see what he was up to beneath the simple phrasing of his words. "He's after you, silly," said my sister in her positive way. "After me for what?" I asked her, and the contempt on her face was unbelievable, "Because he has asked me if he could keep my drumstick it doesn't mean he wants to keep me".

"Don't try to be funny," said Doll witheringly, "it doesn't suit you. He wants your drumstick as a memento – there hasn't been a wild rush of souvenir-hunters round you up to now!"

Then she added under her breath, "Why did it have to be you?"

I could not believe it. I would not let myself believe it. Then
he sent me a large box of violets from Cornwall, and he wrote
his next letter to me in such a way that there was no doubt what-
soever that what my family suspected was actually true.

> I love you, Sylvia, and have always done so and always will,
> but there are two barriers against me. One is that I am not
> literary like you and I have not the same intellectual accom-
> plishments; and the other is that I have to make periodical visits
> to the East. These two barriers always loom up whenever I
> think of you, Sylvia, but if you do not think them insurmount-
> able I should love sometime to talk things over. If, on the other
> hand, you think they are too large, I don't see the use of us
> meeting.
>
> That is all I have to say, Sylvia. I am not a good letter-writer
> and put things very crudely but the substance of it all is that I
> love you – love you too much to ever cause you pain.

I was at that time seventeen years of age: my parents acted with
grim decisiveness.

My father had bought a property in Perthshire. The house was
a gay, pink-washed, low-lying building broken up into small
towers and minute lattice windows. The remains of an old
Roman camp coiled through the grounds and gave the house its
name.

It was here that I was taken and hidden. Much as my parents
wanted to see me respectably married, they considered that this
stranger from the Far East, the son of the woman my father so
bitterly disliked, was not a suitable husband for me. Sarawak
seemed to them as ominous a future for me as if I had been sentenced to Siberia. They pictured it scorched and desolate, with
naked savages swarming in the jungle and clinging to the blackened branches of the trees, when they were not lopping their
enemies' heads from their bodies. They imagined me, shrivelled
and hideously tanned, returning to them at intervals of three to

five years – or else headless and buried in the barren soil of the north-west coast of Borneo.

I was therefore banished to "Roman Camp", and forbidden to write or communicate with Vyner Brooke. My mother did everything she could to direct my interest to other things. Our Scottish home was beautiful. The river Teith flowed beneath the drawing-room window and salmon and brown trout could be caught from its banks. The garden had green lawns and small paths which led to the river's edge; there was a crooked wall-garden in which grew abundant fruit. Over the other side was a mound of purple heather where my parents built a little house for me to write my stories in, undisturbed.

Sometimes I would go fishing in the brown burns, up Ben Ledi with a basket of sandwiches and a bottle of beer. I would walk for miles, fishing, and dreaming, and wondering. Would Vyner forget me in his isolation? Would he ever write to me again?

My mother and I were having breakfast one morning in the cool green-walled dining-room, when some letters were brought in. I looked up disinterestedly and suddenly saw the familiar grey envelope with the small handwriting sprawled over it. My heart began to thump. I could hardly breathe and I felt a flush spread up my face. Fortunately my mother was so eagerly searching for a letter from my father, who was staying at Balmoral with the King, that she did not notice this one. She did not see my scarlet cheeks or the way I snatched up the letter. Only the butler saw and gave me a sagacious wink.

In those days it was the fashion for demure young ladies to wear beneath their skirts rough serge bloomers that gripped respectably below the knees with strong elastic. Cautiously and with considerable difficulty I squeezed the precious document through the elastic and felt it flop softly within the voluminous folds of those abominable knickers. When my mother looked up she saw her composed and docile daughter eating eggs and bacon without, apparently, a care in the world.

"Reggie is all right," she said with a sigh of relief, as though she expected to hear he had suddenly been beheaded by Royal command. "Did you get any letters?" So innocent a question – but her dark eyes were probing and suspicious. "No," I replied, "why should I? Nobody ever writes to me."

It was so easy to deceive my mother, even while that letter was burning in my bloomers. She had never had any cause to lie to the man she loved, but fear makes liars of us all and I was very fearful of being found out. As soon as breakfast was over I ran to my room and lay on my little low bed. My heart pounded, my hands trembled as I read Vyner's letter over and over again. This really was a love letter. Whatever happened, he said, he would wait for me – centuries if need be. He could not understand why I had not been to see him. He was sailing for Sarawak the next day. He had sent me some violets; and signed himself "Yours always, a true friend." That was all.

Just those few frantic lines meant that I, with all my homeliness and ill-fitting clothes, had gained a lover. I kept saying to myself, "It must be my sister really. He can't possibly mean me." I sat down and began to write to him. I wanted to say so much. I thought of all the stories I had published and tried to weave some of their romance into my first love letter; but somehow any flowery language seemed out of place for this simple honest man who had said so candidly what was in his heart. I eventually smuggled to the post office, not the masterpiece I had hoped, but a clumsy ill-expressed scrawl that I was ashamed of the moment it had left my hands.

It all seemed so unreal to me – the Ranee Margaret, the orchestra, her three sons – everything seemed like a dream now. The ordinary routine of my life had been shaken by this shy unobtrusive man. His timidity filled me with dismay. "I love you, Sylvia," he had written, "and have always done so and always will." Surely that should have been enough; but the fear of my parents dragged at my heels, their disapproval of Vyner and their constant insinuations that anyone living in the Far East was an undesirable maniac with indescribable habits. Because he occasionally had a few drinks, he was, to them, an incurable alcoholic. They probably believed that he had had innumerable native

THE GREY FRIARS ORCHESTRA
(seated at piano, the Ranee Margaret; seated left, Dorothy Brett; seated right, Sylvia Brett)

ENRICO CARUSO (*left*) and J. M. BARRIE (*right*)

women. To them, all men living in that insufferable climate were consumed with sex, their morals drowned in the jungle pools and scorched by the eternal sun.

I felt incapable of going against my parents but for my sister it was different. She saw herself held prisoner at home and wrote passionate appeals to the Ranee Margaret to save her from the suffocating influence of her family. The Ranee, bewildered and a little bored by this onslaught and yet flattered by her adulation, wrote to my father. "Doll turns up everywhere," she said, "I never know where I will find her. The other day when I opened the little food trap that leads from the kitchen to my dining-room expecting to find a nice leg of lamb, there smug and smiling was your daughter, Doll." Infuriated letters flew to and fro between "Orchard Lea" and "Grey Friars".

When I heard from Vyner again he sent me of all things a perfect silver model of my own big drum which he had so often tuned for me. On the top of it he had had inscribed in his own hand-writing "From a friend". I still have it beside me on my bed-table; and even now when I look at it, it stirs my heart because it was characteristic of him, so quiet and reticent, yet so romantic.

As the months passed, Vyner, the Ranee, and Grey Friars began to fade a little from my memory. If it had not been for my one love letter and my little silver drum, they might have been a dream. When at last Vyner was expected to return from Sarawak, my sister asked me, "What are you going to do?"

"Do – about what?"

"About Vyner, of course," she replied, "you've got to do something, haven't you?"

Perhaps she was right – but what? Should I propose to him, as I had to J. M. Barrie? Should I remind him of the letter he had written saying he would wait for me for ever? My sister had received many letters from him; perhaps he had said the same to her.

As soon as Vyner returned to Grey Friars, the orchestra was reorganized, but it was not quite the same somehow. I never had one moment alone with Vyner – but the Ranee Margaret, my sister, and he were always together. My fears and suspicions seemed all too well founded – as, indeed, they were.

It was a wet day, I remember. Rain poured from the dark pines on to the damp earth. Grey skies, with no sign of breaking, stretched everywhere. There had been nothing much for us to do at Grey Friars; and the Ranee Margaret, out of mischief, suggested that Vyner should go into the next room where my sister was sitting, and propose to her. She gave him a beautiful enamel necklace that she herself had designed and made. She told him to go into the Blue Room where he would find Doll seated in a cretonne-covered chair. "Give her the necklace," the Ranee said, "and ask her to marry you." She laughed and kissed him and pushed him towards the door. Vyner has told me so often of this little scene that I can visualize it as if I had been there.

He went into the Blue Room fully prepared to ask Doll to be his wife, but, because she was not sitting reading in the chair but was standing by the bookcase selecting a book, Vyner panicked and entirely forgot the purpose of his intrusion. Thrusting the necklace into Doll's astonished hands he muttered a few unintelligible words and fled from the room.

7 *An uncollected parcel*

IT WAS AFTER THIS that Vyner seemed definitely to make up his mind to marry me. He took my sister into his confidence and between them they worked out a scheme; while I went about mechanically, powerless either to act or think for myself. Doll used to invent some reason why she and I should drive into Windsor, and the real reason was invariably Vyner, lurking in the doorway of some hotel.

I was in my little attic room one day, pasting photographs into an album, when my sister came in, trembling and excited. She locked the door behind her and stood leaning against it, staring. "Are you prepared to run away?" she said slowly.

"Run away?" I repeated stupidly. She drew a letter from her pocket and began to read it.

> Dear Doll, arrange that THE PARCEL is delivered at the 'Squirrel Inn' where I will collect it in my car. I will then take it away with me as arranged. Vyner.

So they had planned it all behind my back! I, THE PARCEL, was to have no say in the matter. I was simply to be delivered and collected. I was helpless with indecision, and I cannot imagine anyone more irritating than I must have been at that moment, standing there with my mouth open and an empty suitcase in my hand. Yet as I listened to Doll I caught a little of her fervour; I

forgot my father and mother, and I forgot my fear. Rushing
hither and thither, I packed my few belongings. I often laugh
when I remember the contents of that small brown bag; severe,
simple, and unlovely was that runaway trousseau of mine. A
brush, a comb, a toothbrush, a pair of blue serge bloomers and
one stiff-boned corset.

The Squirrel Inn was about a mile and a half from "Orchard
Lea", on the other side of Windsor Forest. As I ran, the trees
seemed to be lowering down on me, and the branches barring my
way; I slipped and slithered on the clumps of moss and fallen
leaves; soon my shoes were sodden, my clothes torn and soaked.
It was like a nightmare as I went on running with the brown bag
flapping dismally against my legs, running on into nothingness,
uncomprehending and afraid.

I arrived at the Squirrel Inn, my cheeks scarlet, my damp hair
hanging in lank strands over my eyes – to be met by the landlord
with a message to say that Vyner was not there. His car had broken
down; and I was to hire a car and drive at once to his mother's
house. I was shown into a little private sitting-room to wait until
Mr Tombs, the driver, was ready. That wait was my undoing.
Had Vyner been there we might have been married five years before we eventually were. But he was not there; and suddenly I
realized the enormity of my situation. All my doubts came flood-
ing back. Suppose his car had not really broken down? Suppose he
also had lost his courage, or that this had all been forced upon him
and was more than he could bear? Suppose – suppose – my nerve
snapped, and clutching the brown bag, I ran headlong from the
inn, back down the forest path, back to "Orchard Lea" and up
the corkscrew staircase to my room. My sister stood over me calling me a fool, and I sobbed and sobbed and could not stop.

*   *   *   *

Vyner took the failure of his plans with philosophical good nature,
and just before he sailed for Sarawak again he sent me an enormous basket of violets from Cornwall, and wrote:

I hope you will forgive me for being a nuisance to you in the past. The more I think of it the more convinced I am how very selfish I have been in the whole matter. Anyway I can't bother you any more as I sail tomorrow. Your always true friend, Vyner Brooke.

So for five more years I was a spinster in the Parish of Winkfield, and during that time my parents took me, with my tears and my heartache, to London, and tried to divert my thoughts by immersing me in a new world of literature and theatre. It was thanks to them that I met nearly all the most famous actors and actresses of the time. I was grateful, but not cured. I was merely licking my wounds and dreaming of the only man who had ever told me that he loved me.

Why had I turned back from that runaway bid for freedom? Why had I no feeling for myself, for him, or for my parents just nothingness, as if everything inside me was asleep. While I had been in the orchestra I had never asked myself if I was in love with Charles Vyner Brooke. I had only thought of his mother, with her heavy masculine face and compelling eyes; and this was precisely what she intended. She wanted her sons to take wives but not to love them: it was necessary for them to marry to safeguard Sarawak, but her whole will fought against sharing them with her daughters-in-law. She was a desperately jealous woman when it came to her sons. In a way, we knew this. We knew that though she pretended to care for us, it was only for one purpose, yet we could not entirely refuse her.

A few months later I heard that Vyner was dangerously ill. He had been out fishing in Sarawak in a small open boat and the rain had poured down on him all day. A mere chill developed into an abscess on the liver, and for weeks he hung between life and death. He was given the Last Sacrament, but thanks to his physical fitness and determination to live, he slowly recovered. At last he wrote to me, telling me that he would be back in London at the end of the week, and could I meet him?

I felt breathless, as if the earth had suddenly shaken under my feet. I knew the hour of decision had come. This time there would be no plotting and planning over which way and where the "PARCEL" should go. I showed the letter to my father.

I shall never forget his reply. "This is a charming letter," he said. "He seems a nice fellow. Why don't you see him?" If only he had said that five years earlier.

So after all these years of separation and despair and frustration, I was at last allowed to see my lover alone.

8   A delayed proposal

WE MET at Prince's Restaurant in Piccadilly. I do not know who was more terrified, he or I. He seemed paler and thinner after his illness but there, still, were those incredible blue eyes, the fine Brooke nose, and that determined chin. We had a strange, shy luncheon. I am not quite sure what I really expected – perhaps that he would fall on his knees in the middle of the restaurant and declare his passion for me. However, the word "love" was not mentioned. Instead he began to tell me how he had once been locked in a lavatory and unable to attend a party with his mother and the Empress Eugenie.

My sister was waiting for me at the top of the stairs when I returned home. "Well!" she gasped, "Did he ask you? DID he?"

"We had a discussion about lavatories and plumbing," I replied miserably and burst into floods of tears.

A week later, Charles Vyner Brooke, Rajah Muda of Sarawak, asked me to be his wife.

He very nearly didn't. I had a hole in my stocking, and he told me afterwards that he was so mesmerized by the sight of my naked heel protruding out of my shoe that he almost forgot to propose. Vyner's sense of the ridiculous worked like that. In conjunction with his shyness, it was liable to rob him of his purpose quite alarmingly, as had happened with Doll. However, this time all was well.

The excitement over our engagement was tremendous. The Press dipped deep into their stock of clichés for the occasion, and I hardly recognized myself. I had American blood; I was a well-known author; I was Viscount Esher's beautiful daughter, petite, clever, and enchanting; and I was to occupy an Oriental throne.

Of all the letters of congratulation I received, George Bernard Shaw's was the most amusing, and utterly characteristic:

I'm not at all pleased to hear that you are in love with somebody. You ought to be in love with me. That is the usual thing and I think the proper thing at your age. I hope the other fellow is married or in some other way put on a high shelf, because it is not wise to marry a man you love, it makes you a slave and a nuisance and the poor wretch cannot live up to it, whereas if you love somebody else you have a husband with whom you can be at your ease and you can have your dream all the same without ever waking. There should always be another. He will keep well if you take care to keep him imaginary. Your husband can have another too, on the same conditions. As long as he is any sort of a decent fellow, one husband is as good as another. It takes six years to learn to live together, and get over the most furious fits of wishing you hadn't married him, and hating him, but after that he becomes a habit and a property and you stop bothering about it.

You are quite right about old buffers being the most interesting. When I was your age, I would not look at a woman under forty. I defy you to find a young man half as interesting as I am. But you cannot enter into enduring relations with old people. Just think of it; I am just thirty years older than you. I was forty-four when you were fourteen. We should have met then. I was still beautiful. Now you are twenty-four (unless that is a whopper of yours) and I am fifty-four. Relations are still possible, if a little forcedly paternal on my side. At thirty-four, you will be much more business-like and I will be sixty-four. Well, what of that? Goethe was a fine man and Ibsen a crusty one at that age. At forty-four you will be in your prime. A splendid female. I will – I mean I shall be seventy-four. You will give instructions that you are not to be at home when I call, though you will be very kind when we meet and you can't avoid me. At fifty-four you will have begun an active and interesting part of your life; and when someone tells you she saw me yesterday, you will say; 'Good Heaven! Is that old creature still alive? Why, I was at the theatre with him thirty years ago and he was an old man then. He must be over ninety?'

You must be provident in these matters. People are always changing into something else; that is why enduring relationships are such chancy things. You will have to pick up some unripe young man who will disagree with you; but then you are unripe yourself and will disagree with him. You really ought to have got it over and laid in a lapful of babies by this time. After that, nothing matters; one settles down to business and realities but here again you have to look ahead. Children grow up and then they want mothers, not grandmothers; don't you go imagining things if I don't write. I ought never to write a line outside my work. If you could read shorthand, like my secretary, I could send you reams; as it is my wife watches me jealously every time I take out my pen. Not from jealousy of you, but from jealousy of my health, for she knows it is bad for me to write after dinner, which is just what I am doing now, so I shall stop.

G.B.S.   To Sylvia.

It was gay and fantastical and very worldly-wise, but it wasn't much help to me. Thanks to the distance between my parents and myself, I was both innocent and ignorant. I once saw a letter that my father had written to his favourite son on the subject of love:

Remember, love is an art and that one of the artistic things is not to tear a passion to tatters but to establish a reserve even if it does not exist. I know this is hard but beware of the danger of excess, even in affection. Let the beloved one have an occasional hunger for you, as you for her, and be not too prodigal of favour. You see the difficulties and the obstacles which the conventional world places in the way of your free intercourse. 'Stolen fruit' and numerous other ancient adages are singularly true.

Two things destroy love which is based on a foundation of passion. One is the absence of reciprocal feelings, the other satiety – both kill – no love is strange, it is all, in whatever guise, so very human. The friendship of a schoolboy is as full of tenderness and jealousy and passion as ever love itself.

This was a side of my father I had never known. All I remembered of him was his cold and critical grey eyes and the power he had to create a man and to destroy him. My brother Maurice could bring out the best and the worst in him, and how much suffering and sweetness there was between these two no-one will ever know.

What my father said to me about my engagement was, "If a man marries he brings his wife into his family, but when a girl marries her husband takes her away from her home for ever."

All this did nothing to allay my fears or pacify my trembling heart, or prepare me for the dreaded, unknown actualities of marriage. I wrote to Vyner to tell him I did not feel I could live up to his love for me, to which he replied: "I will not have you say things against yourself. You are the most beautiful being in all the world to me and I am your slave for all time."

How long I had dreamed that a man would feel that like for me, and yet, when it happened, I could not believe that it was true. I plagued him with letters beseeching him to tell me that he really loved me. Patiently he wrote back: "You are on a pedestal, darling, that I look up to with a kind of reverence in my most human love as I consider you so much higher and better than a poor mortal like myself. I often wonder how it can be that you, such a wonderful person, so charming and gifted could be happy with a chap like me, moody, undemonstrative, and un-intellectual."

As a boy, Vyner had been taken straight from Cambridge and plunged into a little outstation in the interior of Sarawak called

Simmanggang, there to learn the duties of a young cadet in the Sarawak Service. The old Rajah's school had been a hard one, but there had been justice in it and wisdom and immense foresight. He wanted his eldest son to know the nature and extent of the Brookes' rule in Sarawak, so that, in the fullness of time, he would be properly equipped to inherit it. Vyner had had his share of warfare in Sarawak. He had led several expeditions into the interior to subdue certain tribes of head-hunters. He had marched on the famous expedition when, out of a force of ten thousand warriors, two thousand died of cholera round his camp.

This was the man, a hero in my eyes, who said he loved and admired me. Can you wonder I needed reassurance?

The banns of our marriage were published in the Parish Church of Braywood. It still seemed fantastic and unreal. It was only a little while ago that I had run through the forest with my dilapidated brown suitcase filled with nonsensical trifles, including a black and white checked sponge bag containing a bar of soap I had stolen from my mother's maid's room. Now I was surrounded by dressmakers, forever shopping for frocks and frills, lingerie and lace, for my expensive trousseau, and about to marry the eldest son of the world's only White Rajah.

My brother Maurice was also in the news. He had resigned from the Coldstream Guards in order to marry the actress, Zena Dare. Society whispered and nudged and raised its aristocratic eyebrows: what did it matter? My father snapped his delicate fingers in the discomfited face of convention; but Society was undeniably shocked.

My elder brother, Oliver, was in New York and rumours reached us that he also had found his anchorage. Now all of us were settled except my sister, the bravely independent girl in her boyish attire and short haircut, who was incapable of doing anything, in the eyes of our mother, that was either dutiful or right.

Before my wedding I went for a week to stay in the house where we were to spend the first night of our honeymoon. There I met Mr Asquith, who was, at that time, Prime Minister. I remember sitting with him in a little summer house by the side of the river while we discussed life and literature and the art of writing. "When I prepare a speech", he told me, "I sit in a room packed full of information. Have your facts at your elbow – have everything round you – dictionaries, dates, quotations, and above all a Thesaurus. Never use a word more than once, if you do it lessens its strength. The English language, you must always remember, will sound like an organ if you play it well."

My mother, Vyner and I spent the night at a small hotel in Oxford in order to see the University. Long after everyone was in bed I heard a knock on my door. Cautiously I opened it and there was my prospective bridegroom, standing in his shirt-sleeves and carrying his boots in his hand. He looked just like a man who had come to read the gas meter – but that was not by any means what he had in mind.

"What do you want?" I asked him.

"You !" he replied with a grin. He was always more a man of action than of words.

Majestically I pointed to the door. I was not that kind of a girl, I said. We often laughed about it afterwards. "You know what, Mip," he said, "you made me feel I was trying to break into the nursery and rape the baby instead of the nurse."

He told me later that it had been uphill work courting me because of some kind of barrier I seemed to have built up between myself and the rest of the world. I could not tell him what I felt; only in letters could I show him glimpses of my love for him. "Are you happy, darling?" he kept asking me; and I could only answer, "There is no word in any language to express the way I feel."

I remember my father's definition of Elysium in his journal: "Happiness only comes by the way. Its direct pursuit is a forlorn business. It is so hopelessly futile. There is only one unforgivable vice – CRUELTY – I do not care whether it is towards animals or human beings, there is no real line of demarcation – this is the philosophy of life and the secret of happiness."

Wedding presents began to roll in. King George V and Queen Mary gave me a pale blue enamel brooch with pearls round it, and their initials "G and M" in diamonds on the face of it, surmounted by a crown; Queen Alexandra gave me an enamel brooch with the name "Alexandra" surrounded by diamonds. J. M. Barrie sent me a set of his works, and Sir Ernest Cassell, who was a dear friend of mine, a gorgeous sapphire and diamond bracelet. Vyner presented me with a dressing case filled with gold brushes and bottles and boxes, and a bright red car I called the "Scarlet Sin". Vyner had spent so much of his youth in Sarawak that very few people knew him, and he received so few presents that I mixed them with mine so that he should not feel embarrassed!

We were married at St Peter's Church, Cranbourne, on 21 February 1911. It was a bleak, damp day; and as I put on my wedding dress of ivory satin, and arranged the wreath of orange blossom in my straight dark hair, it seemed to me as if my soul had left my body and was standing watching this small sallow bride with her sombre eyes and awkward elbows. Between that girl and myself there was the shadow of a suppressed and morbid child, who had twice tried to destroy herself; and I seemed to hear a voice saying, "I am still here, you know. You won't be able to get rid of me just because you are being married. You haven't defeated me yet."

As I walked up the aisle on my father's arm this feeling of separateness, of not belonging to myself, persisted. We passed a Boy Scout Guard of Honour and a throng of excited villagers who pressed and pushed to see what was going on, and then my father was handing me to my equally agitated bridegroom.

During the service I could scarcely breathe. This was partly because my dress was too tight, and partly because of the violent beating of my heart. All my old, dread doubts came back at that moment and suffocated me. Suppose, at the last minute, some Malay woman stepped forward with a baby in her arms, the offspring of one of my husband's early indiscretions? Suppose he did not really want to marry me, but had been driven into it by my sister and the Ranee Margaret? Suppose—suppose—. But these were not the terrors of Sylvia Brett, the twenty-four year old bride of the heir apparent to the throne of Sarawak; they were those of the doubting, unhappy little girl who had shed so many tears in that ivy-papered lavatory; still insecure, still afraid that happiness could never be hers.

For the reception at "Orchard Lea" an immense marquee had been built out into the garden. Among the throng of guests was Vyner's father, the old Rajah, who had been dragged unwillingly to the marriage of his son, didn't know who his host was, loathed the whole affair, and only wanted to leave as soon as possible. He turned to the first man he saw, and said, "How the hell can I get out of this damned house?" The man happened to be my father, who was so astonished that he meekly showed him the door.

When the time came for us to leave, Vyner had disappeared. The guests became uneasy; one or two tried to be funny and said that of course he had run away; for a bleak moment, all my fears flooded back; then a resonant voice rang out over the babble of talk, "The Rajah Muda has lost his trousers!" A few moments later, Vyner emerged, very red in the face, but with his lower limbs decorously covered.

We left in a shower of rose petals, and drove straight to Nuneham Park. I dare say I was not the only woman who, on the way to her first night of marriage, thought: "In a few hours I shall be in bed with a man I hardly know, and I haven't the faintest idea what is going to happen to me." People who protest that modern literature leaves nothing to the imagination are welcome to the horrors that mine supplied me with on that drive.

When I undressed that night, my trembling fingers would hardly unfasten my clothes. I put on my bridal nightgown of pale pink chiffon and lace, and looked in the mirror, to meet my own terror-stricken eyes and chalk-white face. Was this the kind of woman, I wondered miserably, to arouse passion in a man? Dismally I climbed into the enormous four-poster bed, and the sound of my husband's approaching footsteps was like the beating of the executioner's drum.

The following morning I hardly dared look at Vyner. He made one of his funny faces and said, "Well, that's that, now we go on to Rome."

9 *A difficult birth*

VYNER had lived in Genoa when he was very young, and Italy, he had decided, was where he would spend his honeymoon. We went first to Genoa and then to Rome.

I soon discovered that my husband was an indefatigable sight-seer. Unfortunately his only guide book was so old that it might have been used by the ancient Romans; its information was out-of-date or incorrect, or both; we found ourselves at museums that had long ago been turned into apartment houses or had ceased to exist. This merely amused Vyner, for he was a man who positively preferred things not to be perfect. He liked cars that broke down, electric lights that fused, houses with primitive plumbing. He refused to consult a time-table or book tickets in advance; so, on our travels, we just used to sit at railway stations and wait for a train to come along. It was on our honeymoon that I learned what patience meant. He would never let me know where we were going, as he wanted everything to be a surprise. Thus I would find myself let in for a long walk in high-heeled shoes, or clumping round some famous art gallery in hob-nailed boots; but it was impossible to be annoyed with him; he had such gaiety, such sunshine of the mind.

"Aren't you glad you came, darling?" he would ask, as, panting and perspiring, I trailed up stone steps and along stone corridors looking at endless lines of fabulous paintings. But it was a rhetorical question. How could I tell him that I hated museums and did not understand medieval art?

In the evenings we would drive to the Ponchio and watch the lights of Rome being gradually lit. It was so beautiful, I wished he would make love to me then and there. Instead, he regaled me with anecdotes from a little book of jokes he had bought and learned by heart in order to amuse me.

I often smile to myself when I think over those early days with Vyner. I had been so brainwashed with sentimental books that I expected my honeymoon to be a marvellous romance that I would remember for all time. I haven't forgotten it; but it wasn't quite as I'd imagined. My husband said to me once, "You know, Mip, there is no such thing as love. There is passion, and there is friendship. When a fellow is first attracted by a woman it is her body he wants more than her mind. If he marries her just for that, it won't last. But if he says to himself, 'Now there's a girl I can get on with, she's fun', though he may not know it, he has laid the first foundation stone of a perfect marriage."

I learned in the years to come how right he was.

From Rome we went to Sorrento. The little hotel hung enchantingly on the side of a cliff so covered with flowers that it looked like a gay bouquet flung down from the sky by God. There were days splashed with sunshine and nights with Italian singers under our window. There were high walls with cactus like giant octopus, and the sea like a deep blue apron stretching as far as the horizon. Vyner even forgot his book of jokes, and it was here that my first child was conceived.

We went to Capri and Venice. There the weather changed and it became damp and chilly. Many of the gondolas so glamorously described in Vyner's out-dated guide book had been replaced by small motor boats that shrieked and hooted their way through the calm canals. One of the things I remember most vividly about our somewhat lengthy honeymoon is the Italians themselves, who pinched my bottom as I climbed the dome of St Peter's or window-shopped in one of the streets. I resented this intensely, but Vyner said I ought to be flattered.

As soon as we left Venice, I began to feel sick. No-one had ever told me about the symptoms of pregnancy. I became moody and irritable; all the things I most loved about Vyner, his cigar, his shyness, his ringing laugh, I now found jarred my nerves. Then one morning I heard two old women talking on the stairs. They were nodding and smiling and pointing at me. The honeymoon had been too long. I told Vyner, and we packed our bags and returned to England.

Among the letters waiting for me when we reached Stanton Harcourt, our new home, were two from my "literary godfathers". J. M. Barrie's was only a note, in his usual gentle, rather sentimental vein; G.B.S.'s began:

> Ride a cock horse
> To Sarawak Cross
> To see a young Ranee consumed with remorse
> She'll have bells on her fingers
> And rings through her nose
> And won't be permitted to wear any clothes.

I don't know what you call it, Sylvia, but I call it simple unfaithfulness.

> For 'tis oh my heart is left, Lady
> to find myself bereft, lady
> of Sylvia, my left lady
> For a heathen potentate.

Ought to be ashamed of yourself, you ought. Look here, will you come to lunch at half-past one on Friday and bring the heathen potentate? You should introduce him to the intellectual side of London. I mean, of course, to me. I know the notice is short, but I couldn't help it. You can leave the potentate behind if he is bashful or otherwise engaged. G.B.S.

Vyner did not accept the invitation. Although he was one day to become ruler of a country, this, to him, was simply his job; the prospect of having to meet somebody famous sent him straight into his shell. The instinct was so strong that if such a person called at our home, Vyner would literally lock himself up in a clothes cupboard, and stay there until the visitor had gone. Yet he played cricket with the village team, and was happy and at ease with the local farmers and tradespeople. He even had the vicar to tea. It was my "highbrow friends" that scared him; and I remembered how in awe of me and my father's brain, which he attributed to me, he had been. He preferred simple people, and was warmed by their admiration.

When the time approached for my baby to be born, Vyner rented a house in London, No. 8, Cadogan Gardens. How well I remember every corner of it! My bedroom looked out over the gardens and in the tree-tops three over-fed pigeons cooed contentedly. It is strange that during my whole life with Vyner we never had what we felt was a real home except in Sarawak. In England we always hopped from house to house, like uneasy birds who had landed on strange soil. So it was in a rented London house that Leonora was born – prematurely. It seemed that I was too small-boned to go my full time and give birth naturally as other women did; but I had as gynaecologist Sir Henry Simson, and it was his knowledge and skill that enabled me to bring three children safely into the world. Nevertheless, for me, childbirth invariably meant long periods of torment and delirium, as my body was torn and abused in the interests of creation.

After three days of labour, a little baby weighing three pounds or so, was delivered. She was not red and crumpled as other babies are, but was a bundle of pink and white perfection like a painted doll; and like some precious doll, she was wrapped in cotton wool. Vyner and I gazed at her with unbelieving eyes. We had done this, he and I. He showered me with flowers, and was in the seventh heaven of delight.

My father-in-law was in Sarawak when Leonora was born and was not at all pleased when he heard I had produced a daughter. I knew that he had prepared elaborate ceremonies in honour of a first grandson, with bell-ringers standing by to peal forth the joyful news. It was the thought of those bell-ringers, that prevented me ever giving birth to a son and heir. I could visualize the grim old Rajah sitting in his palace, his glass eye glittering as he tapped the floor impatiently with his stick; and the Chinese bell-ringers hanging on the bell ropes, waiting for the signal that never came. It was enough to put anyone off.

I had once written to Barrie and suggested that he should be the father of my children; now I wrote and asked him if he would be Leonora's godfather.

When my daughter was eight months old, Vyner said that he must go back to Sarawak. This was the moment I had been dreading: should I go with my husband or stay with my child? Men need their wives, and Vyner, especially, needed me; but my baby was delicate, and her life at that time hung on the thinnest of threads. Whatever I did, I felt that I was in danger of losing one of them; yet Leonora, I reasoned, was too young to miss me; and I desperately wanted to be with Vyner, and I desperately wanted to go to Sarawak. It was, after all, my husband's beloved home. Shutting my mind, I decided to accompany him.

10 Sarawak at last

IT WAS on that first voyage out to Sarawak that I really began to know my husband. He would sit by my side on the ship's deck and tell me about himself. During the course of these conversations, he revealed a side of himself that I never dreamed of, and I listened, wide-eyed.

To put it mildly, he was a man who was quite incapable of resisting women. "You know what I like about women?" he said to me, "I like to look at them and say to myself, 'will they or won't they?' The funny part of it is that if they don't I'm furious and if they do I'm bored."

"Did you think I would?" I asked.

"Not for a moment," he said, laughing, "but it was damned well worth trying."

One of his best stories was of an amorous escapade he had had in a Japanese brothel. He had gone out one evening with two friends and all three had got comfortably and demoralizingly drunk. It was the fashion at that time in Japan for the little Geisha girls and their customers to make love encased in a sack. Two of the girls were dainty and small, but the third, Vyner's, was a buxom beauty called Sugar Plum. Vyner himself was by no means a spindling; he was burly and broad-shouldered, and he was very drunk. Try as he would, he could not get into the sack with Sugar

Plum; and half the night was spent in thinking out ways and means of solving the dilemma. Finally they gave up in despair; Vyner fell in a stupor on to the bed and, Sugar Plum slept alone in the sack.

I realize now that, in his honest way, he wanted me to understand his weaknesses as well as his strength; but how artless I must have been to have imagined for one moment that this old leopard would, or could, ever change his spots.

Vyner was very apprehensive that I would not be happy in Sarawak, but he need not have worried. As long as I live I shall never forget the moment we turned from the sea into the Sarawak river, and saw the broad and winding beauty of its pale brown water. The little villages were clamped on to the mud banks as if the palm-leaf houses had been tumbled from a basket and left exactly where they fell; coffee-coloured women stood waist deep in the water with their long bamboo jars upon their shoulders; and children, too young even to walk, dived and swam among them like little brown tadpoles. There were tangled mangrove swamps along uncultivated banks, and behind them rose the real jungle with its majestic trees and monkeys swinging from branch to branch. There was something fearsome about the richness of this ancient foliage in a land of mysterious legends and beliefs; and yet, as I gazed at all its luxuriant beauty, I knew that a long dark chapter in my life was ending. My childhood was over at last, and I was home.

When we sighted Kuching it was about midday; and then I heard the beating of many gongs. The river banks were lined with people, and, as we passed the Fort, the great gun fired a Royal Salute. With its echoes still rolling, we anchored close to the Astana steps. Crackers were fired and more and more people were gathered along the front of the bazaar. A company of young men, each carrying a Sarawak flag and dressed in neat white uniform with a coloured sash and a black and red velvet head-dress, was drawn up on the river wall facing the Astana. They sang a long welcome to us in Malay. Spread across the sky was an enormous yellow banner:

WELCOME TO THEIR HIGHNESSES,
THE RAJAH MUDA AND THE RANEE MUDA

Mr Caldicot, Resident of Sarawak proper; Mr Baring Gould, Resident of the Third Division, and Mr Dallas, the Treasurer, came on board to meet us. They looked serious as undertakers and almost as depressed as they viewed with unconcealed amazement my inadequate five feet; no doubt they were remembering the majestic beauty of my mother-in-law, the Ranee Margaret. In complete silence we made our way towards the Astana. A Guard of Honour, under the command of Captain Cunningham, was drawn up on the lawn, and as we passed, they presented arms. The Rangers' Band blared forth the Sarawak National Anthem. Slowly, amid a thousand watching eyes, the Rajah Muda, heir to this incredible inheritance, walked up the stone steps of the Astana, while I followed four paces behind him, as custom demanded, for as well as being his consort, I was his slave.

The Astana Palace was a fantastic medley of beauty and bad taste. Outside, its walls were white and it had a grey tower where a sentry stood on guard day and night. Inside, tremendous rooms stretched the whole length of the building. There was nothing wrong with their proportions; but the old Rajah had filled them with appalling imitation stuff from every period of English and French history. Cheap gilt stood side by side with poor mahogany. Early Victorian sofas rested stiffly against the walls. Crude Dresden figures held caskets in their chipped and broken hands, and mirrors were dotted about on thin-legged tables. Only the ceilings were beautiful. They were heavily carved with gorgeous dragons and wide-open flowers of plain plaster, designed and executed by an ordinary Chinese workman. With Oriental furniture to match, the palace would have been a masterpiece instead of a travesty. In the dining-room was a gleaming table made of native billion wood, and on the walls were portraits of James Brooke and Charles Brooke but none of my husband. He firmly refused to join that family group.

We slept in gigantic cages on hard beds with a Dyak mat on

them. We had a reading table and a light; and it gave me a wonderful feeling of security when I closed the door of my cage. No mosquitoes, no wandering animals or creepy-crawly things could nestle under my pillow. It did not matter if bats flapped against the wire netting, or soft enormous atlas moths fluttered noiselessly outside. Safely we lay on our austere and simple beds, listening to the tree frogs with their never-ending love call. There is a certain bird in Sarawak whose full-throated song, softer than a flute, makes my heart stand still even now as I remember it. It is called a "bubet", and is somewhat like an English blackbird, only fiercer.

People speak of the silence of the East. Sarawak had no such silence. All day, hawkers plied their wares in the bazaar, gongs beat in the mosque, and, now and again, one heard the wailing of a one-stringed instrument lingering in the air. At night there was the eternal chorus of tree-frogs, bull frogs, and strange beetles. Often this clamorous chorus would swell into a million tiny sounds until it seemed that every leaf, every flower and every blade of grass possessed some living thing that was calling to its mate. The magic of it all possessed me, sight, sound, and sense; there was in this brilliant and abundant land everything for which my heart had yearned.

11　*A tyrant's return*

VERY SOON after we arrived in Sarawak my father-in-law returned from a trip into the interior and our days of freedom and fun were at an end. The government officers shivered in their shoes, the smiles on the faces of our Malay boys had gone. It was as if a curtain had been drawn down upon the sweetness and contentment of this idyllic land. I had only seen him for a moment at my wedding and I had forgotten how starkly supreme he was, how gaunt and unapproachable; a stern figure with a hawk-like nose, one glass eye from which a constant trickle of water dripped on to his snow-white moustache, and a heart of stone.

Charles Anthony Johnston Brooke was born at Berrow, near Burnham in Somerset, on 3 June 1829. He was the second son of the Reverend Francis Charles Johnston and Emma Frances Brooke, sister of the first Rajah. He was educated at Crewkerne Grammar School and at the age of thirteen, inspired by his uncle's adventurous example, he entered the Navy as a volunteer in the sloop *Wolverine*. Later he was transferred to the famous *Dido*; and it was in this ship that he first came to Sarawak.

His early training at sea might well have widened his vision and expanded his nature; but it had the opposite effect, driving him deeper into himself, and freezing him into a cold discipline and a rigid uprightness. "My nephew is too damned serious for me,"

James Brooke would exclaim with a twinkle in his eye, "or else I am too damned frivolous for him."

Charles joined the Sarawak Service when he was twenty-three. He was appointed to an out-station called Lundu, one of the loneliest in the land which afterwards became a sort of punishment fort to which our officers were banished for any misdemeanour. There was nothing there except a few native huts, fruit trees, and an immense waterfall that tumbled noisily down through the jungle. The Land Dyaks looked upon him with shyness and fear. He had none of the easygoing ways they were used to in his uncle. He was awkward and pompous, ill at ease and unable to assume James Brooke's hearty manner, ready hand-shake and the genuine affection in his eyes. Charles was hopelessly and pitifully British, chilly, aloof, and totally unable to express himself.

In the meantime James had become anxious about the future of Sarawak. He had no son and did not feel absolute confidence in either of his nephews. At one time he even went so far as to leave his country to his closest friend, Baroness Angela Burdett-Coutts; but changed his mind. He finally wrote to his eldest nephew, "My surrender of authority is final, and you must take up what I am forced to leave."

But when the time came for him to leave Sarawak, he positively refused to renounce his throne. Sarawak was the very breath of James Brooke's body; but his eldest nephew only saw him as an obstinate old man determined to cling to power as long as he could. He informed his uncle that he wished him to tell the people of Sarawak that he was the lawful heir. "I shall be grateful if you will publically install me as Rajah Muda," he wrote. "Not only will it be a pleasing sign of your confidence in me, but it will strengthen my hand in carrying out the government."

This letter was his undoing. It infuriated his uncle, who was already ill and ageing; and he looked round for yet another solution to the problem of succession. There was still his other nephew, Charles Johnston, who was already in the Sarawak Service, and who, unknown to the old Rajah, had changed his name to Brooke anticipating that something like this might happen.

Once more James Brooke altered his will; and thus Charles Anthony Johnston Brooke became Rajah of Sarawak on 3 August 1868. He was then thirty-eight years of age.

Charles Brooke had not been in the least afraid of his uncle; indeed he was not afraid of anyone or anything. As soon as he came to the throne he set about the task of firm and unbending government. He knew that before the arrival of his uncle, pirates had made yearly trips round the coast, attacking peaceful villages, killing old men and children and carrying away many people whom they sold as slaves in the Sulu Archipelago. He knew there were tribes who sacrificed slaves in order to propitiate evil spirits: for instance, to ensure good luck to a chief's new house, the first post of the building would often be driven through the body of a young virgin; and when a tribe was afflicted by an epidemic it was still the custom in many places to sacrifice a young girl by placing her in a canoe and allowing her to drift out to sea with neither food nor water.

James Brooke had done everything in his power to abolish these practices, but he had been only partially successful. In letters to England he had written:

> The tribes of Seribas and Skrang are powerful and dreadful pirates, who ravage the coast in large fleets and murder indiscriminately. They are the most savage of the tribes and delight in head-hunting and I would like to wipe them from the face of the earth.

It was after this letter that Mr Gladstone launched an attack on James Brooke and a political conflict raged over his head. The disloyalty of the British Government towards him embittered the Rajah and he was never again the gay, even-tempered ruler of former days. From the pages of his famous Diaries comes the cry, "I have at last a country, but oh, how ravaged by war, how torn by dissention and ruined by duplicity, weakness and intrigue."

This was the situation which Charles Brooke had inherited, and he took up single-mindedly the work left unfinished by his uncle.

It was strange that two such different men should have shared such similar ideals, to free the slaves and put down head-hunting, but it was so. James Brooke who was bluff and kindly and affectionate towards the underdog, and Charles Brooke who concealed every emotion and suppressed his very soul, both worked towards the same humane and lofty end.

When the latter returned to the Astana he seemed to me almost inhuman; yet, this icy martinet with his basilisk's glare had a dignity so profound, such intensity of power, it was not surprising that the Malays and Dyaks looked upon him as the very mainspring of the country.

He was deaf, especially when he did not want to hear something. He rarely spoke unless it was to issue an order or contradict a statement. His romantic approach to women was phrased in French – nobody quite knew why. He was Spartan in his habits and would always sit on a high wooden chair or on a bench, and he slept in a narrow iron bed. "Don't believe in fripperies," he would bark, "damned effeminate. Never relax and your stomach will stay where it should be; good for the organs to remain upright."

He had lost his eye by galloping into the branch of a tree, while out hunting at Cirencester, in England. Vyner used to tell the story of how he was walking in London with him one day and had said to him, "Father dear, don't you think it is time you got yourself a glass eye?" The old Rajah, in a particularly jovial mood – at least, jovial for him – replied, "You are quite right, my boy; let us do it at once." They happened to be passing a taxidermist at the time. The Rajah stalked in and bought himself the first eye he saw. It happened to be one destined for a stuffed albatross, and it gave him for ever afterwards the ferocious stare of some strange solitary marine bird.

Whatever may be said of the Second White Rajah, his people knew that he had dedicated his life to them and that he kept faith with them. He would not allow commercial or industrial developments, but encouraged and extended agriculture and education. These alone, he thought, would give these gentle people, so unready for progress and civilization, a firm foundation for the future without destroying their sense of values. He never forgot the fundamental dictum: "Sarawak belongs to the Malays, the Sea Dyaks, the Land Dyaks, the Kyans and all other tribes, and not to us. It is for them we labour, not for ourselves."

We had not been in Sarawak more than a month before a storm began to gather between Vyner and his father. At root it was that resentment of the old towards the young, of the ruler towards his successor, that had incensed James Brooke against his eldest nephew. Now, a generation later, the old Rajah regarded the Rajah Muda with the same illogical jealousy; he would glare at Vyner with his one tormented eye, and weave his schemes to belittle him. James Brooke had had a second nephew to play against the first; Charles Brooke had two other sons; and while he was still Rajah he could leave the country to any one of them, for there was no law that it must be the eldest. He had no real reason to disinherit Vyner, and so the plan he conceived was subtle; Vyner should be the future Rajah, but certain control would be held by his younger brother.

Without even informing my husband of what was in his mind, Charles Brooke issued the following proclamation:

> I, Charles Brooke, Rajah of Sarawak, do hereby decree that my second son Bertram Brooke, heir presumptive to the Raj of Sarawak in the event of my eldest son, Charles Vyner Brooke, Rajah Muda of Sarawak, failing to have male issue, shall be received on his arrival in the State of Sarawak with a Royal Salute and honours equivalent to his rank. I further decree that he shall be recognized in future by all the inhabitants of Sarawak as being part of the Government of the State and such recognition shall be duly registered in the records of the Supreme Council of the Raj of Sarawak.

I do not think Vyner would have resented this so deeply if his father had taken him into his confidence and prepared him for the Proclamation: done as it was, it seemed an open insult. It was a direct statement of Charles Brooke's distrust of his eldest son; and a definite and final assumption that I was incapable of producing a son and heir.

Vyner was furious – I never saw him angrier – yet, throughout it all, he kept his sense of humour. Letters rushed to and fro between the Astana and the Offices; and Vyner, with an enormous pair of field glasses, would judge their effect by the number of people scurrying about like angry bees whose queen has been destroyed.

His first letter to his father was controlled and carefully expressed, but it stated firmly his disapproval of the Proclamation. The old Rajah immediately replied that he was "surprised" at his son's letter and there was only one word to explain it – "jealousy".

In response, Vyner emphatically denied any motive beyond defence of his own and his family's rights; and he went on:

> ... if you persist in giving my brother Royal Honours on arrival, and on issuing the Proclamation and on proposing this new Bill, I shall be reluctantly obliged to make a public protest against your action, and to leave this country until things are more satisfactorily arranged. The position you propose to put me into must inevitably degrade me in the eyes of the population, and amounts to admitting that you do not consider me fit to govern this country without the sanctions and approval of my younger brother. This is a position which I decline to hold. I hope to hear by return that all these proposals, including the reception to my brother, will be reconsidered.

Never in his life had the old man received such a letter. For years his word had been law. That his son should now oppose him, was more than he could accept. He wrote:

> As your letter reiterates your disobedience to my commands, I hereby officially inform you that in consequence of these acts, I give notice that I shall not in future require your service in the Government Offices nor in the Supreme Council. I regret that I feel myself obliged to take up the matter in this way, but

obedience to the Rajah has heretofore been the rule, and will be so long as I am RULER.

You will have no more duties to perform in this country; I recommend your leaving as soon as convenient.

I am, Sir,

Yours faithfully,

C. Brooke, Rajah.

Enclosed with this official letter was a private letter as well, written in his own shaking hand, dated 10 June 1912:

Dear Vyner,

At the same time as sending my official letter I may tell you that I had intended this to be my last visit to the East, and being doubtful if I should be able to conduct affairs of State satisfactorily with you, I had almost decided that I would resign with a few conditions . . . and leave it to you to hold the Raj with your present title until after my death. The conditions would be that I should continue to have power over the Treasury; and the concessions in my name, Brooketon and Panduruan, are not to be disturbed without my sanction. My retirement would be, of course, reported to the British Government and I should be clear of responsibility in future. Whether the Interior will be safely managed or not will then depend on you. I shall go up on my coast trip to bid goodbye to all friends, old and new. I only wish you success in the future. The reception of Adeh will be as the Proclamation sets forth.

Yours faithfully,

C. Brooke.

PS. What I should recommend you to do would be to travel, and the transfer of Raj could take place after my return in September. I have no ambition for myself personally, and my only consideration is for the safety of the future. I came into power after the late Rajah's death under very different circumstances forty-four years ago.

Vyner saw at once that, despite the difference in tone, this letter altered nothing. The old man intended to overcome opposition by ignoring it. The only thing to do was to go back to England and await events. For the first time, he had dared to oppose his fearsome father. I felt I did not know the man I had married, for here, beneath the gay smile and genial manner, was a will of steel. It was a side of him that neither I, nor many of the Government officers, had ever seen before. The alarming correspondence between father and son shook Sarawak to its foundations; not even James Brooke's dismissal of his eldest nephew had created such a stir.

I had seen nothing of the country beyond a few formal receptions at the Astana and the Resident's house, and a display of fireworks given by the Tamil community which, owing to dampness, had failed to ignite. I had met very few of the people. I pleaded with Vyner to stay, in the hope that the storm would blow over, but he replied, "My father never changes his mind and neither do I."

It must not be thought for one moment that my brother-in-law was to blame. He sincerely believed that Vyner had been informed of the Proclamation and had agreed to it. Bertram Brooke, or "Adeh" as he was called, had worked quietly and inconspicuously back in England on Vyner's behalf, demanding nothing for himself and seeking no praise. There could not have been a more straightforward or kinder man than Adeh or a stronger supporter of the Raj. He knew nothing of what awaited him on his arrival in Sarawak.

Both Vyner and I had left letters for him, and they were not very pleasant. Vyner explained why he had gone. He was uncertain as to what part Adeh had played in the formation of a State Committee in London, of which he had been made the President. "I am to do the dirty work out here," Vyner told his brother, "whilst you and your gang are to say what I am to do and not to do. No thank you." Then he added, "I do not return to Sarawak again unless with full power. By full power I mean absolute control over the country." All I can remember about the letter I wrote is that it was rude beyond all reason.

Poor Adeh! Anyone more innocent of duplicity could not have been found; and never at any time had he been other than a faithful friend. Now that I look back upon those times I can see that it was not really the fault of the Second Rajah. He was a fine old man, but he could not realize that his sons were every bit as loyal to Sarawak as he was, and that the great Brooke tradition would be safe in their hands. The mistake he made was in not trusting his eldest son; of, if you like, not giving him the benefit of the doubt; and no man of Vyner's mettle could accept the throne under the conditions he imposed.

JAMES BROOKE

CHARLES BROOKE

12 *England and war*

So, while Vyner and I returned to England, Adeh arrived in Sarawak and was welcomed with a Royal Salute and a Guard of Honour. He was introduced to the Supreme Council by his father with great pomp and circumstance, and proclaimed Heir Presumptive.

By now my second child was well on the way. "Don't tell the old Rajah," I implored Vyner, "or he'll line up those damned bell-ringers again." However the newspapers got to know that, once again, Sarawak was "expecting"; the old Rajah summoned his bell-ringers; and I brought another daughter prematurely into the ancestral line. Down went the flags in Sarawak; the festivities were cancelled. I could picture my taciturn father-in-law as he sat in the oppressive heat, waiting for a grandson to be born; and the letter of congratulation he wrote me was, to say the least, somewhat stiff.

When he came back to England and established himself at Cirencester, I wrote and asked him to forgive and forget our unfortunate visit to Sarawak. I begged him to be friends again with his son, and assured him that we had not meant to be disloyal or ungrateful. The whole incident, I said, had been a regrettable and unhappy one for us all. He replied at once, suggesting that we let bygones be bygones, and inviting us to stay at Chesterton House.

It was unfortunate, from my point of view, that the old man's suspicions now included my family; he had got a bee in his bonnet that the Eshers and the Bretts were plotting to give Vyner full control of Sarawak. It showed how little he knew his easy-going son, or of my father's dedication to the English throne. Had Adeh, the Tuan Muda, been a conniving and ambitious man, he could have made Vyner's position as an autocratic ruler impossible; but he was not; and in this Vyner was very lucky.

We went to Cirencester all the same. The house was like a taxidermist's nightmare, or a sportsman's Nirvana; foxes' masks and brushes, whips, spurs, and hunting horns, were everywhere and the whole place smelled of bran and oats. Every passage was hung with emblems of slaughter. I wouldn't have been surprised if the tropical birds the old Rajah kept in his aviary were there for use as targets.

I learned a great deal about my father-in-law during that weekend. I discovered that his own sister was so much in awe of him that she dared not call him by his Christian name. I was told how he met and married the Ranee Margaret. Bleak and cold and calculating, he had courted her in spite of the fact that he was in love with her mother. I could picture him in his frock-coat and tall hat, driving to their country house at Warnford Place in Wiltshire. There, to the strains of one of Chopin's Nocturnes, he had stiffly placed upon Margaret's knee a scrap of paper on which he had written the following bit of doggerel:

> With a humble demean
> If the King were to pray
> That you'd be his Queen
> Would not you say nay.

Margaret had tried hard not to laugh. Her mother had arranged the marriage; to Margaret herself, it had seemed a suitable match, and something of an honour to be wooed by this frosty, unapproachable man. There was certainly nothing romantic about it.

Now that we had two children, our flat in Davis Street was too small, and Vyner began to search for a house. He found one, at last, on Wimbledon Common. It was called "Tilney", which was why he took it. He thought it would remind me of the little street where I was born and where my parents lived for so long. No sooner had we settled there than I received a letter from Bernard Shaw in his most impish vein:

Sylvia,

Do not tell me reproachfully that your last letter to me was dated 18th September, and that the day-after-tomorrow will be the 18th of October. I know it; and I reproach myself more than I deserve. I have been travelling meaningless thousands of miles, breaking my car and getting it mended; being on fire and putting it out; scorching and unpacking and packing and paying and tipping with frightful vicissitudes of energy and high spirits and emptiness and despair. I rested only at Southern places where I could feel nothing and write nothing. When I came to life in the North I could only go to bed tired, or to a cinema or drift about strange streets and rivers in the moonlight. This is my last night abroad, and I consecrate it to you.

Touching that perverse female infant, I quite realized that its sex was an Oriental tragedy. When the necessary boy does come he will be so bullied by older sisters that he will probably inaugurate his reign by cutting off every female head in Sarawak. And there is a still more awful possibility. My mother began with two girls and finished with me. To make a man of genius you require practice. You practise on girls, say two girls, and then having formed the habit of making girls, when you try a boy you start him as a girl before you recollect what you are about, and only get his sex in at the last moment, with the result that he is a monster who writes plays because he can be a hero or a heroine on paper just as he chooses. Having begun with an infinitesimal you will end up with an immortal; and that will be a very stormy outlook indeed for you and Sarawak. The sooner Vyner hands that unhappy country over to the British Government for thirty million or so, the better. Then you can hand the immortal over to his doting grandmother to be spoiled, and live happily ever after.

But women make the best Sovereigns. The Salic Law is not a man's job; it is a woman's. The relation of a King to his ministers is intolerable; the relation of a Queen to them works out much better or else a King ought to have a female Cabinet.

Are you up yet? You ought to be; but the modern mother who can afford it is kept in bed and fed up until her bed becomes a mere lake of milk. If she nurses the baby, it becomes a weakling for life; if it is stodged with food or the like, it becomes powerful and healthy beyond its years. Female invalids always complain, 'My mother thought it her duty to nurse me.' Moral, nurse only if you find it voluptuous – and give the baby a good dinner afterwards.

I cross to Folkestone tomorrow and go for the week-end to my rectory at Ayot St Lawrence, Welwyn, Herts. On Monday I must come to London, as I have a lecture to deliver. I am open to inspect Elizabeth as an excuse for conversing with the parents she has disgraced. Have you seen "Androcles"? It's an ideal play for children; but I doubt if it will run until Elizabeth is advanced enough to be taken to it.

G.B.S. Boulogne sur Mer.

16th October 1913.

Tilney House was plain-faced and suburban; squat and low gabled, with big bow windows that looked out over Wimbledon Common. My life at that time was filled by my two babies. Leonora was delicate, very nervous, sensitive and intelligent. A slight cast in one eye gave her a timid, trembling look; and she would have fits of screaming that nearly broke my heart. Elizabeth was different. She was completely square, like a soft pin-cushion. Whichever way you put her she remained there entirely relaxed. Her hair was black and hung thickly round her ivory face. Her eyes were enormous; one was flecked with grey like a collie dog's, and its sight has never been entirely clear. She had sweet ways, and so much affection; while Leonora seemed shy of any display of emotion, just like her father. Whenever I laughed she would hit my arm and scream, "Stop! Stop!" as if my laughter hurt her.

It was extraordinary what terrors pursued her. The doctor said it was because she had been brought into the world prematurely, and that in time she would grow out of them. I sent J. M. Barrie her photograph so that he could see what kind of a godchild he had. He wrote and thanked me in his usual pedantic way:

My dear Sylvia,
Thank you so much for Leonora's photograph. It is a dear face and she already looks as if she knew most of the things that are worth knowing. WHAT THEY are I have no idea and that gives her a grand look of mystery.

Only too soon the time came for Vyner to return to Sarawak, and once again I had to face the breaking-up of our home. I thought by then that I had it all worked out. Whilst the children were still young, I should have to content myself caring for them, and learn to bear the separation from Vyner. It was easy enough to decide this while he was with me; but the moment he left, I felt utterly alone; and I resented the captivity of motherhood. "You've got *us*, Mummy," the children would say wistfully, and they would look half-frightened, as if suddenly aware that they were not, by themselves, enough. I hated being responsible for that look in their eyes; but I could not help it. I longed so much to be with Vyner.

I did not know until after he died that he had kept so many of the letters I wrote him during our first parting. When I re-read them I realized how cruelly disturbing they must have been to a man who put his duty to Sarawak before everything else.

Remember you are most of my life. [I told him.] Without you the world has no meaning, the sun has no warmth, and the very rains and winds are nothing to me. I wanted our love to be the most perfect, honourable and faithful thing. I wanted you to live in me and me in you for ever and ever. People tell me that I should never have let you go out to Sarawak alone and that you will soon find some other woman to console you. But

I am completely confident that you will never leave me and I try not to listen to anything they say. Marriage isn't a prison is it, darling? I think that each one of us should learn to live alone. I think one of the finest words in any language and within any living soul is FREEDOM.

I gradually became used to my solitude; the stricken anxiety left my children's faces; and I began to reconstruct a little of my old life, and the slender chains of friendship I had made. I had lunch with my dear old friend, Sir John French, and we discussed every subject under the sun. He was easy to talk to, and a perfect companion, with his changes of mood from gaiety to gloom.

A few days later I went to a ceremony at Windsor Castle with my father, and he introduced me to Lord Kitchener, for whom he had an almost fanatical admiration. After his death aboard the cruiser *Hampshire*, my father wrote of him in his Journal:

Certainly nothing can be meaner than the way our people have used Kitchener's great name to suit their petty political exigencies. He lies peacefully at the bottom of the seas, un-heeding these jackals. . . . No-one among his colleagues realized that he had no axe to grind and cared for nothing except to see England victorious. It is right and proper that he should be made a scapegoat for men who had an eye on "honour" or their pockets. It is all in the great tradition of heroes and martyrs.

Early in August I took the children up to Scotland to "Roman Camp" where my father and mother and Zena, my sister-in-law, and her family were staying. Rumours of war with Germany were rife. Sir John French came north to see my father. He had been warned that he would be put in command of the B.E.F., and he was deeply pre-occupied and worried. His eyes were shadowed as he paced up and down the garden with his hands behind his back. "This is too much for me," he said; "I don't like it, Sylvia, I tell you I don't like it one damn bit." I tried to assure him that he was well fitted for his new post, and that anyway, the war would be over in a month. That was what we all thought then, even my father. "I will do my best," Sir John French said, "but I doubt very much if my best will be enough." It was indeed hard for this cavalry leader, who had fought so gallantly in South Africa, now to find himself dragged from his simple soldiering into a world-wide war, and forced into a conflict not only of weapons but of words.

My father was in a turmoil of organization, flashing like a meteor from the King to the Army, from the Navy to the Flying Corps, dispensing wisdom. Many were jealous of him, for he had no scheduled work and was not bothered by red tape. Lord Esher may not always have been welcome, but they had to admit they could not do without him.

The effect of the war on Sarawak reached me in letters from Vyner. His main fears were profiteering and a shortage of rice, which would have meant revolution. However, a thousand bags came in from Singapore, and seven hundred bags of flour; and, owing to Vyner's excellent management and the enthusiastic co-operation of his Government officers, things adjusted themselves, and the danger of panic was averted.

Meanwhile I took over an empty house in Callander called "Inverleny" and turned it into a Military Extension Hospital for the sick and wounded. We were attached to the 4th Scottish General Hospital at Stolehill, Glasgow. There were twenty-one beds in my little Extension, and we had cases from fifteen different British regiments and from several units of the Belgian Army. My sister-in-law and I were active members of the Voluntary Aid Detachment of the British Red Cross, and we were also members of the hospital's governing body. Zena was much more capable than I, as the sight of blood made me violently sick. I finally resigned from the nursing department and banished myself to the pantry to wash dishes. In the evenings I played the piano and organized concert parties. The only trouble I had then was with my nurse's apron, which had been made for a taller woman, so that the red cross which should have been over my bosom lay instead upon my stomach.

Later I added to my responsibilities by becoming a member of the Callander Belgian Refugee Committee. It was a pathetic sight to see this little group of lonely strangers walking about the town. They sang sad little songs with a plaintive lilt and the very young boys had beautiful voices. What became of them I do not know, for when Vyner returned to England I gave up these activities, and my nursing home went on without me.

Vyner refused the comfortable jobs which my father offered him. He tried to enlist in the Army as a Private, but as he was over forty and had only half a liver he was not accepted; he then joined an Anti-Aircraft Battery stationed on top of the Cannon Street Hotel, but dropped a belt full of loaded cartridges from the roof to the street below, which so un-nerved him and those around him that he resigned. After that he was taken on at an aeroplane factory in Shoreditch, turning out steel fittings on a lathe. Nobody knew him. He was just "C. V. Brooke", a man as tired and grimy as all the others, and he loved it. He enjoyed the friendliness of the other factory workers, who often helped him out and saved him from getting into trouble with the inspector. He never got home till late in the evening, his hands begrimed by oil and dirt and his body aching from standing so long.

His younger brother, Harry, had rejoined the Lancashire Regiment; and Adeh, when he returned from Sarawak, rejoined the Gunners and lectured and trained young soldiers on their way out to the war. Both my parents were doing arduous work in France; my brother Oliver was at the War Office, and Maurice was Provost Marshal of Paris. My sister Doll was befriended by Lady Ottoline Morrell and stayed with her in Oxfordshire.

On 2 December 1915, my last baby was born. Damn, damn, damn those bell-ringers – for of course it was a girl. I remember Sir Henry Simson flinging up his arms in despair because he knew it was the last child I would ever be able to bear. We called her Valerie Nancy. She was lovely, and had tiny ringlets all over her head like feathers. She was born at No. 9, John Street. This time no letter came from the old Rajah; but I did get one from Bernard Shaw:

My dear Sylvia,

This is ridiculous. It is very noble of you to try and make up for the waste of the war at this rate; but there are limits. You are always having babies. It would not matter in Sarawak which ought to be peopled entirely by babies of yours running about in the woods naked; but such tropical luxuriance is rash in London. Don't exhaust yourself. No doubt you, the mother of the "infinitesimal" are the irresistible, but you MUST learn to defend yourself.

I have been on the point of writing to you lots of times during the last eighteen months; but my work exhausts my capacity for forming sentences on paper. And now that I do write I have nothing to say except that I am in the country and can only send you a little play which is not very amusing unless you can hear the brogue in it and know what my countrymen and women are like. . . . Where do you live now, when you are not scattering infants about? . . . Always respected princess and ever dearest Sylvia,

Your devoted, G.B.S.

A little later he wrote again but only upon a card:

Don't ask me to write or even think until rehearsals for my play are over. I have had to write three plays within the last few months in the intervals of doing other things, and I am dead, beyond speech and almost beyond motion. . . .

When I was well enough I tried to persuade my husband to come out and meet some of my friends. I wanted them to see how handsome he was and how much charm he had, and people had begun to ask why I hid him away. Was I jealous of him, or what? But Vyner would rather have plunged into a roaring volcano to an instant death, than meet a roomful of strangers, and suffer the slow torture of convivial society.

"I can't take you," he said. "You have your father's brain. I want to be left alone. I like being alone. I am never bored by myself or with myself."

"What has my father's brain got to do with going out to dinner?" I asked him.

"Talking," he replied. "Knowing how to talk and what to say." No-one knew better what to say and how to say it than my husband, but he would never believe this.

I finally induced him to come with me to a dinner party that Millicent, Duchess of Sutherland, was giving at her home across the Common. The whole time he was dressing he was cursing and swearing and groaning and mumbling. "This is awful, Mip," he complained. "Can't you say I've been suddenly taken ill? Damn it, I AM ill, I think I am going to be sick. Suppose somebody is rude to me. Suppose they are all rude to me?"

"People don't ask their neighbours to dinner in order to be rude to them," I replied coldly; but I wished that there had never been a Millicent, Duchess of Sutherland; and that we had never come to live on Wimbledon Common; and that the world was empty except for the Rajah Muda of Sarawak and myself.

At dinner I was seated exactly opposite Vyner and was in a state of speechless paralysis, wondering how he would behave. At first he seemed to be profoundly bored, and then quite suddenly he came to life and I saw him gazing at the woman next to him as if hypnotized.

"What had she got?" I asked him on our way home.

"What had who got?"

"That woman you never took your eyes off. I thought she was singularly plain."

"Plain!" he replied with that joyous laugh of his, "she was a monster; but damn it all, Mip, I could see right down her dress!"

I never dragged him out to dinner again, because he threatened that if I did he was going to take off his trousers and make a scene. He much preferred to stay at home with a book. He would read for hours at a time, often long into the night, and he remembered all that he read. He regarded everyone connected with Society as a snob, and preferred to be with simple people because he understood their thoughts and how they felt. He never forgot the part of his childhood in the Earl's Court Road when his family had been very poor. Then, his only pleasures had been watching the trains go by, painting the front door of the house, and sitting in the gallery at some music hall and spitting on the nobs below.

The war went on and on; it seemed it could never end, but it was time for Vyner and me to prepare for our second visit to Sarawak.

13 Back to Sarawak

AT FIRST it was arranged that my sister would accompany us, but, characteristically, she changed her mind at the last moment.

Then, one night when we were out at the theatre, we met Doris Stocker. She was in the chorus of the Gaiety Theatre, and later married the famous breaker of speed records, Sir Henry Segrave. Vyner asked her on impulse if she would like to come out to Sarawak with us; her caustic sense of humour appealed to him. I had already begun to learn how much he needed the affection of a pretty girl, and how the good opinion of others compensated him for the poor opinion he held of himself.

There was no room for us at the Astana when the old Rajah was in residence, so we went to stay in a separate bungalow. This, as you may imagine, was no hardship to us, as he was hardly a genial companion at the best of times. If only he had been able to express to me the merest hint of the poetry of the country, its broad brown rivers and fertile soil, its teeming fruitfulness. But all he was interested in was economic facts, so many acres of rubber trees and sago swamps, pepper gardens and rice fields; so much per bushel – so much in the Treasury. These were what consumed him, order, straight dealing, hard work; whether it was fish to be controlled, speared, and collected; planting, or road mending, with the prisoners chained together as they worked. There was no room in his grim world for the hibiscus or the orchid, for lolling in the sun, or a siesta in the shade; no room for poetry. Inefficiency was anathema; he did not spare himself, and he did not spare others, either his Government officers or his Malay and Dyak chiefs. He would not let the industrious Chinese take advantage of the other, less shrewd races. "To each his own", and let no man covet his neighbour's land, his longhouse or his wives – though Charles Brooke was not averse to desiring a few of the latter himself. He looked upon himself as God's gift to women, and bleakly wooed his loves in his hard and toneless French.

Each week there was a dreadful ceremony called "The Band Day", when we all dressed up and gathered round the old Rajah on a stretch of grass. The Police Band would play classical music, and we would respectfully listen to the discordant sounds which were the best that they could produce, and which he, of course, could not hear. His favourites would sit on either side of him, and at intervals would scream some trivial remark into his ear, while he beat time on the ground with his stick. We dared not leave until the Band had laboured through their repertoire, and sat there, devoured by mosquitoes and pouring with sweat. I think he took a perverse pleasure in our discomforts: if we did not like classical music – even that played by the Sarawak Police Band – we damn well ought to.

Sometimes he would take me for a drive. He had imported a spirited pony from Singapore which he drove in a diminutive dog-cart. We invariably ended up in the ditch; but, quite unperturbed and with considerable dignity, he would drag pony and cart on to the road again. "A little frisky today" he would say, thoughtfully regarding the bucking pony; "No vice, just wants to play."

Palace Receptions were even more of an ordeal than the Band concerts. He would invite the entire Kuching community, Government officers and their wives, Malay chiefs and their wives, and the principal Chinese, not because he was anxious to see them but from a sense of duty. Guests knew before they arrived that the sooner they left the better. Vyner and I would stand behind the

Rajah and help him receive the nervous and reluctant guests who filed up the stairs towards us. There would be a little small talk on the veranda; drinks were offered round; and once more the Rajah's favourites would flutter to his side like butterflies, their shrill voices and unnatural laughter intended to convey to those who were *not* his favourites what a wonderful time they were having. Hot and agitated, I would move from one group to another with a fixed grin on my face; while Vyner would get as far away from his father as he could, and every now and again I would hear his laugh ringing out, as out of place, in that solemn palace of gloom, as a jester at a funeral.

The men were divided from the women like sheep from goats, so we would sit in a row on iron benches that paralysed our bottoms, and talk in thin whispers to one another until dinner was announced. During dinner our tongues were loosened a little by the wine, and the Rajah's favourites could be heard screaming, "Yes, Rajah", "Oh no, Rajah", "Do you really think so, Rajah?", as playful as kittens. There was no electric light in the Astana in those days; and as we sat on the veranda with our coffee and liqueurs, the hurricane lamps flickering and spluttering in the breeze drew a horde of monstrous bats, and hard black beetles which hurled their shining bodies against our naked arms. Then, quite suddenly and without a word, the Rajah would rise to his feet and move to the head of the stairs. There he would stand with his hand impatiently outstretched, and his guests knew that they had the signal to leave.

Charles Brooke had a remarkable habit of relieving himself over the edge of the veranda during these parties. Once, in a lull in the conversation I said in my loudest and clearest voice, "Listen, it's begun to rain." There was a stricken silence, and turning my head I saw the old autocrat, ruler of fifty thousand square miles and half a million people, standing up quite unashamedly before his embarrassed guests and watering the cannas over the veranda rail.

There was no mixed club in Sarawak at that time. The men had billiards and bowls and tennis courts, and a primitive golf course; while we had to make do with a little wooden bungalow that had

been solemnly dedicated to "THE LADIES". It was without ameni-
ties; there was not even a bridge four; and no men were allowed
up those chaste wooden steps because the Rajah disapproved of
what he called "Damned poodlefaking". But we did have a
small bar, for which we were devoutly thankful, and here we
would sit every evening, five or six disconsolate women, with
nothing better to do than tear our neighbours' reputations to
pieces.

The barrier between the sexes was in those days unbreakable.
The Rajah reckoned that if any man in his service got married, he
lost ninety-nine per cent of his efficiency. If he wanted a woman,
there were plenty of Sarawakians, and girls of twelve or thirteen
were exploited for this purpose by their parents. It was a vicious
doctrine; it drove white men into the welcoming brown arms of
the local girls, involved them in tropical entanglements, and produced a harvest that remained long after they had gone.

We had both Catholic and Protestant missionaries in Sarawak;
the following story concerns a certain Chinese boy called Ah
Chong, who was a very dear friend of mine and in whose family
I took a deep interest.

Ah Chong had been converted by a Roman Catholic priest,
and, among other things, he had been told never to eat meat on
Fridays. At his christening, he had been re-named Peter; and some
time after his conversion I went to visit him. It so happened that
the day was Friday; and as I approached his house, the smell of
roasting pork hung appetizingly in the air. I greeted Peter who,
urbane and smiling, asked me to be seated. As we talked, the fumes
of roasting pork wreathed round us, and at last I could bear it no
longer.

"I hope, Peter," I said, "you are doing everything the good
priest told you?"

Peter nodded. "Oh yes, Tuan Ranee," he replied.

"Not eating meat on Fridays, are you, Peter?" I asked.

"Oh no, Tuan Ranee," replied Peter, looking shocked.

"Today is Friday," I continued innocently, "are you quite sure
you are going to eat fish, Peter?"

Again the little polite smile, the dignified bow of the head. "Oh yes, Tuan Ranee, me quite sure I no eat meat on Fliday."

I looked him full in the face. The Chinese do not like being stared at eye to eye, and down came the full soft lids like pale shutters over the blackness of his eyes.

"There is a very nice smell of roasting pork," I commented, sniffing vigorously; "may I see your kitchen, please?" He led me into the kitchen and there sure enough was a juicy piece of pork frizzling in the pan.

"Peter," I said sternly, "you have lied to me. Not only do you eat meat on Fridays, but you also tell lies." Peter looked extremely distressed; then a beatific smile lit his face.

"No, no, Tuan Ranee, me no tell lies. Me no eat meat on Flidays. The Reverend Priest he get me and my name was Ah Chong, but he splinkle little water over me and he say, 'Your name not Ah Chong any more, your name Peter'. So I get piecie pork I splinkle little water over it and I say, 'Your name not piecie pork any more, your name fish!' So you see me eatie fish on Flidays."

Many people have asked me what Charles Brooke made of his reign, and whether it can be compared with the splendid achievement of his uncle. He came to it during a period of stagnation when Sarawak was in debt and trade was at a standstill. The people had expected much of him which, cold and rigid as he was, he was unable to give. Nevertheless he accomplished much. He raised revetments along the mud banks of the river, and turned the small straggling village of Kuching into an almost model town. Roads were improved; offices, churches, mission schools, and the famous Museum were built, along with a recreation club, a golf course, and a race track. He improved the hospital, and this brought more doctors to the country. He strengthened the Army and turned the Police into an able-bodied force. Sarawak acquired a Bishop as well as an Archdeacon, and a Chinese choir which learnt to get their tongues round Hymns A & M as well as "God Save the King" and "Bless the Name of Brooke". Sarawak was a British Protectorate, and the Union Jack and the Sarawak flag flew side by side. When so much had been done, Charles Brooke looked round with his solitary eye and launched three more schemes – the Waterworks, the Railway, and the Wireless.

The Railway ran ten miles into the interior, and then stopped with a jerk on the edge of the jungle. Here the Rajah believed one day another town would be built, but in fact, only small communities grew up alongside the line. Nevertheless the Railway became a great feature in Kuching, and groups of natives used to assemble to watch the morning and evening trains go by. Every time the shrill whistle was heard the Rajah would take out his watch and grunt approvingly, "On the dot as usual." The noise of the train rattling through the marshes was so unexpected that it made us realize how well the seeds that James Brooke had courageously planted were bearing fruit. Charles Brooke's régime, it seemed, could be remembered as the Reign of Progress.

In his last years the Wireless was installed. I can well remember how we used to watch the mast grow, and it became a kind of monument to this mysterious old man. Half the people did not understand what it was for, but they were fascinated by it, and would bring their families from far away to stand before it, open-mouthed. For many weeks it rivalled the Museum in popularity.

One theory was that it was a ladder from which they might see God, and I was in Kuching when a certain Chinese climbed it under this delusion. It was still unfinished; but up and up he climbed, until he reached a small platform. There he lay on his face beside God. We shouted to him to come down but he was too far away to hear us. After a while he rose to his knees and appeared to be singing; then he stood up and leapt over the edge. The crowd shrank back, and one or two women screamed, as the small bent figure came hurtling down to crash into the soft earth. When they ran to lift him out, only his thin wrinkled legs were visible.

Those of us who were in constant contact with the Rajah could not help feeling sorry for him. All he had ever cared for was Sarawak, and now his time was nearly up. The two White Rajahs, each in his turn, had worked for the good of the people they ruled; and unaided they had brought peace, law, good government, and prosperity to the land. Now, covetous eyes were being turned on the rubber plantations and the oilfield. During the Eighteenth Council Negri, in one of the longest speeches the Rajah ever made, he said:

> I have lived in this country now for over sixty years, and for the greater part of that time as Rajah. . . . Has it ever occurred to you that after my time out here others may appear with soft and smiling countenances to deprive you of what is solemnly your right, and that is the very land on which you live, the source of your income, the food even of your mouths? If this is once lost to you, no amount of money could recover it. That is why the cultivation of your own land by yourselves is important to you, not cultivation by strangers who carry the value of their products out of the country to enrich their shareholders. Such products should be realized by your own industries and for your own benefits. Unless you follow this advice you will lose your birthright, which will be taken from you by strangers and speculators, who will in their turn become masters and owners whilst you yourselves will be thrown aside and become nothing but coolies and outcasts.

This fear of foreign exploitation obsessed the Rajah, yet he could not get the Malays themselves to see it. With soft and languid feet they walked trustfully through life under the Brooke rule, basking in the sunshine and sheltering from the rain. The Rajah understood his people; he knew their entire lack of foresight, their entire trust until betrayed. Would they ever learn to guard themselves, to prepare and to provide?

Charles Brooke did everything in his power to protect their interests during his lifetime; he had seen too many other countries thus caught up in the wheels of progress. He was a strange, lonely figure; separated from his wife, half-estranged from his sons, pacing the veranda of his Palace reading snatches of Molière out loud, or humming some French song. Odd, disjointed love affairs were recorded in his Diaries, amorous incidents in which it was almost impossible to visualize him.

He was very deaf, but not, I thought, as deaf as he liked to pretend. I remember a self-important young Government officer discussing with the Rajah certain Dyak troubles, and the right way to suppress them. As usual the Rajah had not spoken much, but the young officer had been both eloquent and opinionated. He pointed to The Fort where the gun was mounted on the hill and said, "A few shots from that, Rajah, would do those bloody Dyaks good." The Rajah did not answer for a moment, and then he said with a bland smile, "So your mother is still living in Plymouth, is she?"

On one occasion, I remember, a well-known Sarawak couple had been caught misbehaving amongst some wood blocks down by the dock. The case was to be tried the next day and the Rajah would be obliged to go into Court and pronounce judgement. The extent of the immorality was explained to him, the appalling example to others, and so forth. The old Rajah appeared to be listening most attentively; then at the end he said, "I don't care a damn about their morals; what I want to know is what is the damage to the wood?"

After the Wireless had been installed the old man seemed to weaken; it was as if he had forced himself to live in order to see it finished. Yet he still went back and forth between his office and the Astana, and went out riding in the evenings. Then one day he fell from his horse and was carried unconscious to a near-by bungalow. Even then he did not give way. "A little giddiness, that's all," he said to my husband. But the Malays noticed with sinking hearts that he never rode again.

I shall never forget his last address in the dining hall of the Astana. It was a speech to a Malay school at which I was to present the prizes. The Datus (Chiefs) sat around with their hands folded upon their knees and complete absorption upon their faces. A few Europeans were seated upon stiff chairs, and the room was lined with rows of neat little Malay boys in snow-white suits and red velvet caps. Before them stood the old Rajah. His body was so frail that you could almost see through him, yet he filled that room with his tremendous personality. He was at that time eighty-seven years of age; and he had not much longer to live.

14   *Toys for God to play with*

I T W A S D U R I N G this visit to Sarawak that I wrote a
short play called *The Dream of Isla*. I sent it to J. M.
Barrie, who criticized it on the grounds that I had
tried to mix the romantic and the realistic: "The innocent girl and
her fall through too much innocence," he wrote, "a very good
subject, of course, but it seems to me to clash with the other. One
cannot, I think, follow poetry and social reform at the same time,
they won't run together." But he was sufficiently encouraging to
inspire me to begin writing again; and I sat down and started on
a novel.

In Sarawak we always arose at 6 a.m. and went on to our separate verandas; for, like complete Orientals, Doris Stocker, Vyner,
and I each had our separate corners, and only met at mealtimes.
The early mornings were cool, misty, and sweet-smelling from
the awakening flowers. It was easy to write under these circumstances.

This new book of mine was not to be an ordinary novel. I chose
for my theme the journey of an Oriental soul through the Planes.
I had never believed that death was a barrier of separation, or that
life was an insoluble riddle answered only by death. Souls marched
on, and human beings were but toys for God to play with. All
this may sound as if my theme went deeply into the doctrine of
re-incarnation and the transmigration of souls; but "Toys" was

essentially a novel, and I tried to bring my children and myself and our strange connection with the Far East into it. I enjoyed writing it; but I'm afraid it was by no means a masterpiece. Very soon after it was completed I returned to England, leaving Vyner to support his father.

All this time, of course, while I was in Sarawak, I had been separated from my children; and it was wonderful during that trip home to feel myself drawing nearer and nearer to them again. As I entered my own front door I felt quite shy of them – or perhaps it was a feeling of guilt because I had been away so long.

Leonora had grown tall, but was still infinitely timid with the wistful expression that seemed to twist my heart. I could feel there was something wrong that caused her to live so much in a world of her own. I used to call it "Leonora's Half-Way House" and she liked to hear me say that. She did not seem able to keep pace with her imagination.

"They come in crowds, Mummy," she would say.

"What comes, darling?"

"Things," she would reply, and her eyes would widen with awe. Then I would remember my own childhood and the agonies of childish fear that I had lived through and knew so well.

Elizabeth was stronger and more self-assured. If she could not get what she wanted, she would go into one of her "black devil moods", and lie on her face and sulk. As I looked at her, the clock seemed to move backwards and I could see my little brother in a white sailor suit behaving in exactly the same way.

Valerie had become an enchanting bundle of feathery curls, high cheek bones, and wide brown eyes. When I considered my three babies, I realized how good God had been to me, despite the fact that I could never have a son.

The war, which had been in its second year when I had left for Sarawak, was gradually and painfully working to its dreadful climax. There were aeroplanes and anti-aircraft guns on Wimbledon Common, and hundreds of men camped. I used to take the children to Wimbledon Station to see the troops start off for the

Front. We would buy boxes and boxes of cigarettes and throw them down on to the platform.

I had not been home long when I heard that the old Rajah was seriously ill. It had started with a swollen ankle. "Damned nonsense, just a touch of gout," he called it; but the swelling slowly spread from his ankle to his leg. Vyner stayed with him at the Astana and looked after him himself; and at last the sick old man and the strong young one were living together in the vast palace, close to each other, yet infinitely far apart. Sometimes the old Rajah would get out of bed and walk up and down the veranda, dragging his blanket behind him and muttering broken words of French and Malay, a jumble of memories passing before his failing mind. Prayers were offered in the churches and the mosques, and the whole town waited and watched for the flag to be lowered from the Palace Tower. But, amazingly, the old man rallied and recovered sufficiently to be able to return to England. The Malays began to regard him as immortal.

In the meantime, realizing that it might be many months before Vyner could join me, I started to pick up the threads of my life at home. Through Lady Ottoline Morrell, my sister Doll had become one of the "Bloomsbury Set"; which at that time included Lytton Strachey, Aldous and Julian Huxley, Siegfried Sassoon, and Alec and Evelyn Waugh.

Sir John French and I met often, and I set great store by our quiet dinners together. The war dominated our conversation; and I noticed his bright blue eyes were a little shadowed, and his laughter a little dead. I could feel his unhappiness, his uneasiness about himself. Yet he would not change; he insisted that a man should be what he is, and not what my father wanted him to be. "If I have no tact," he said, "it is because I am a soldier and not a diplomat." It seemed to be the fact that he was in disfavour with my father that troubled him most.

Later I went to see my parents in Paris. It was an uncomfortable and extraordinary journey. I was all alone but strangely unafraid. I crossed the channel by night and arrived at Calais at dawn. I visited mysterious and secret places amidst the thunder of the enemy guns. In one little hut, somewhere between Ham and Noyon, I met a charming woman who served out hot coffee and soup to the muddy half-dazed men who staggered in from battle. Not long after I met her, I heard that she had gone into the hut one morning, and raising her head and sniffing, had announced that she smelt death, her death. A few hours later a half-demented soldier had rushed in and shot her.

Sir John French was back in France by that time, and I found him despondent and embittered. He blamed everybody for muddling and bungling the war. His hands were tied by the politicians and by my father; and with a helpless shrug of his shoulders he muttered, "I've done my damnedest, there is nothing more now that I can do." Soon afterwards he was replaced as C-in-C by Douglas Haig. I knew what a heartbreak this would be to the "Little General", and I wrote to my father. I suppose this was interfering and foolish of me; but I did not then know the circumstances behind his dismissal. This was my father's reply:

As for the Little General, I have always understood his pain. It was largely his own fault. Largely that of the popular institution under which we live. There is no infinite patience or any consideration in democracy. William of Orange, who fought splendidly without ever a success, would never have been tolerated in these days. The General loves and hates very like the winds. He is not devoted to me. I know his majestic (not religious) side only too well. I know his philosophy too. All these queer meanderings of his mind are interesting enough, I agree. It is they, and a warm enough heart at moments, that make him lovable. But then he can be and is so unrestrained in violence that one only thinks of him as a tiresome child one wishes to shut up in a dark room. There is no misunderstanding between him and me, it takes two to make one. . . . However, I am glad you dined with him. I do not like to feel that after so many years of friendship a man breaks wholly with the past.

My new novel was published, and the critics were kind to it, calling it powerful, eerie, haunting, and morbid, and observing that the influence of the East was strong upon it. Amongst the many letters of congratulation I received, the most charming was from Algernon Blackwood:

My dear Ranee,

I could not write sooner because I had not finished 'Toys' – I finished it last night and I do not think it fails, for it seems to me a consistent study of rebirth logically carried out and in places really wonderful. The people are alive and real, and the soul of the woman slipping from body to body, is very true and haunting. The way you show her soul in different settings, growing, struggling, yet always the same *au fond*, is excellent; so are her reactions to the various men. Ujido is most vivid, and her return to that jungle bungalow helps the reader and tends to make the idea convincing and coherent. Only one detail puzzled me; when she is reborn into Blissa, what soul occupies Susannah's body? I think one reason you failed to make it an epic is, perhaps, a certain diffuseness which tends in many places to direct attention from the central figure – *her soul*. The story wants cutting remorselessly – the mind of the reader wanders here and there, and power is wasted. I know you must develop your other characters, yet they should be developed with an eye (the reader's eye) on *her soul* as the dominating central controlling thread of interest. It is not enough to mention here and there that Sudarah and Sereni are peering over Susannah's shoulder and peeping up through her mind in vague memories. It has to be shown, not merely mentioned, this struck me.

But the real difficulty, I think, is the subject of re-birth; if it is to grip and move and convince the reader, it must be treated in an immense sort of way. It is immense both in meaning and perspective. The spirit of the Eternities must be your background. Pretty-pretty is the wrong setting; it should be epic, not lyrical. It's an exciting theme, as I found in Julius Le Vannon and "The Waves" where I too invited failure. "Toys" would be better as a long short story, impressionist, condensed, with just enough detail for atmosphere. This is my honest opinion, but the book remains for me the best and most sincere treatment of re-birth I know. I should like to come and talk it over with you when I come to town, if I may let you know. I come up rarely, but I will take my chance.

We never met. A long time afterwards, just before he was due to read some of my short stories over the air, he died.

It was some time after "Toys" was published that I was quite suddenly taken ill myself. I thought perhaps I had strained myself playing with the children, and I did everything I could to deaden the pain. But it went on, and I was forced to send for Sir Henry Simson. He immediately sent me to a nursing home for a minor operation. "Only a few days, and you will be up and about again," he told me.

I was in the nursing home for four long months with some kind of septic poisoning, and nearly went mad with pain. Every joint of every finger was swollen and had to be wrapped up in cotton wool. One of my ankles was locked in a cage to keep it still; I lived on morphia, but nothing could allay the agony of it. Almost worse was the fact that I had to fight it alone. Vyner was still in Sarawak, my parents in France. The noise of air raids and of antiaircraft guns shook my bed, and I felt I would rather die than go on any more. However, after a major operation, I began slowly to recover.

At the same time, the old Rajah, who was staying at the Hyde Park Hotel, was dying; and to cap it all Vyner was seriously ill with dysentery and malaria in Colombo.

On 17 May 1917, Sir Charles Brooke died at Chesterton House, Cirencester. He was buried under a yew tree in the little churchyard at Sheepstor beside his uncle, and a memorial service was held for him at St Paul's. The King was represented; and to the music of Chopin's Funeral March and the Sarawak National Anthem, played by the Band of the Honourable Artillery Company, the Second White Rajah of Sarawak took his place in the fascinating history of British rule overseas. To his vacant throne, my husband, Vyner Brooke, now prepared to step.

Part Two

15 A new Rajah proclaimed

IF ONLY the old Rajah could have heard his son's words on the day that he was Proclaimed, his fears for the future of his beloved country might well have been laid to rest. I was too ill to return to Sarawak for the ceremony, but I read about it in the *Sarawak Gazette*.

A platform was raised on the steps of the Government Offices, and the people gathered below it. Many of them climbed into the trees near by, looking like immense flowers in their many-coloured sarongs. Roped in upon the dais was a space for the Europeans; and in the very centre of the space sat my husband. Amidst an expectant hush he rose to give his people his first public address as their ruler.

His delivery was excellent, apparently; and it amazed me to learn that this shy and retiring man was able to speak in a voice so confident and sure that even the Chinese coolies leaning on their rickshaws, and the Tamils on guard over their cattle and goats, heard every word he said. Speaking in Malay, the new Rajah began his speech:

I make known to you, Datus, Pangirans, Abangs, Inchis, Chiefs, Towkays, and all classes of people in Sarawak, that I will on no account interfere with the Mohammedan faith, or with any other religion or belief of the people. As the white

Labu and the Undur fruit show white when they are split, so too is my heart unblemished towards you.

Gentlemen and Datus of the Council, and servants of the Government, do your duty to the best of your ability and show truth and justice in all your dealings. My people rich and poor need never be afraid. If you are in trouble or have anything to complain of, I wish you all to tell me so that I can help you. . . . Therefore never be afraid to come to me.

I trust that you, gentlemen, Datus, Pangirans, Abangs, Inchis, Chiefs, Towkays, and all classes and nationalities will assist by straightforwardness, justice and truth, to maintain and strengthen the Government of this country.

These sentiments were as reassuring to the people of Sarawak as they would have been to the old Rajah, could he have heard them. Another Brooke was on the throne; continuity remained unbroken: first, James, the Brave; then Charles, the Wise; now Vyner, the Good.

The end of the speech was followed by the playing of the Sarawak National Anthem, and a twenty-one gun salute. One of Vyner's first acts as ruler was to send a message to the King at Buckingham Palace:

I have the honour to inform your Majesty that I have been proclaimed Rajah by the people of Sarawak. I beg to assure Your Majesty of the unswerving loyalty and devotion to Your Majesty of myself and of my people.

The King replied:

Cordial thanks for your loyal and friendly telegram on your Proclamation as Rajah. Congratulations and best wishes for the prosperity of yourself and Sarawak.

Next, Vyner sent for his brother, Adeh, to come and assist him in the administration of the country; and he appointed him a Member of the Supreme Council. Thus, though not quite in the way the old Rajah had planned, the two brothers together gave their services to Sarawak.

In the meantime I had completely recovered from my operation; but the illness had left me with a weakness in one of my lungs, and the doctors advised me to stop in South Africa to convalesce for a month on my way out to Sarawak. It was difficult at that stage of the war for any woman to obtain a passage anywhere, unless she was on active service. However, due to the kindness of the Japanese Ambassador in London, I was allowed to travel on a Japanese transport ship. I was the only woman on board and was regarded as the "mother" of the ship.

After a dialogue by cable between London and Sarawak, I was fully expecting Vyner to be at Cape Town to meet me; but he was not there. This was awkward, as I hadn't a penny to my name; I cabled to Vyner in Sarawak, and a reply came back from the Resident that my husband had left, but his whereabouts were unknown. In despair I wrote to the Governor of South Africa, Lord Buxton, and asked him if he would help me. He could not have been more helpful; he guaranteed my good name at the hotel – the manager had begun to regard me with unnerving suspicion – and later on had me to stay at Government House for several weeks.

There were three floors at the Mount Nelson Hotel. The ground floor was for the respectable, the first floor was for the doubtful, and the second floor was for the thoroughly questionable. I was put on the second, a clear indication of my status in the eyes of the management. I really believe they imagined I had invented my title myself.

I found myself in a strange mood during that interval of waiting for Vyner, as if some deeply-suppressed devil within me was fighting for release; a dangerous mood of relaxation and abandonment. I had never been interested in or attracted by young men before, or felt at all at ease with them; but there was something about being alone in a strange city in wartime that triggered off a recklessness in me. I flirted outrageously; and, of course, it ended with a young man letting himself into my room and announcing that he was going to spend the night with me. Slowly he removed his coat; and then carefully took out his glass eye, which he placed on the mantelpiece, while I watched the performance, quite speechless. Even if I had been the most passionate woman in the world, I could not have sinned before that glittering and baleful orb. While the young man lay sprawled and snoring on my bed, I spent the night on an upright chair. In the morning he put on his coat, put in his glass eye and swept out of the room. Needless to say, he never spoke to me again. Then there was a rather good-looking Air Force officer who turned on me in an explosion of hatred and called me a frigid flirt. He threw me into a cactus bush and it took me a whole day to get the thorns out of my behind.

There was really nothing to be ashamed of in these limited indiscretions, these casual encounters with desire; though they seemed very shocking to me at the time. To offset them, there were happy days surf-bathing at Muizenburg, walking and window-shopping in Adderley Street, and, all the time, that wonderful air doing its healing work on my lung.

Eventually I received a cable from Vyner, from Hong Kong. He cabled me money and said he would meet me in Singapore. I left Cape Town without regret, and with dark memories; of all the interludes in my life, that period in South Africa was the most disturbing, as if, for the first time, I had been brought face to face with the evil side of my own character.

CHARLES BROOKE AND HIS THREE SONS
(Vyner, Harry, and Bertram)

VYNER BROOKE, THE RAJAH MUDA,
AS A YOUNG MAN (*top left*)
and SYLVIA BRETT AS A YOUNG WOMAN (*above and below*)

16 *Home is where the heart is*

YNER met me in Singapore and we returned to Sarawak together. My health had completely recovered, and I was given a wonderful welcome. The town and river were thronged with people, and innumerable native boats, tongkans, and launches gaily decorated with coloured flags, came out to meet us. As it grew dark, these boats were all illuminated, and their colours were reflected in the water. Not until the early hours of the morning did the last light gutter out.

I could not have been given a better proof of the people's affection; it washed the bitter taste of Cape Town from my mouth. I sank once more into the warm arms of the East, and knew for certain that here was my anchorage, here was the country that I loved. For all its ennervating heat, and the perspiring discomfort of any physical effort, I never for an instant regretted the course my life had taken.

I loved Sarawak; and now, when I am old, I can still recapture its patterns as it was when I first began to get to know it. The inner peace that seemed to me to have no outer world, is within me still. The sun rose and the day lazed quietly through the hours. There was no twilight, just a sudden darkness and little lamps flickering amongst the palm trees and over the small town. Sometimes a boat would go by like a black leaf upon the moonlit river with a Malay boy singing to his love; or one heard the distant laughter of a child and the melancholy twang of a Chinese mandoline.

Fifteen miles above Kuching the great rivers divided and branched into smaller streams that wound their way like brown ribbons through the jungle, and both the Land Dyaks and the Sea Dyaks built their long-houses close to them. The Sea Dyaks were the taller and better built. They believed in dreams, and birds were their oracles. Not being able to read or write, they had no literature; but the history of their tribes was expressed in legendary songs and incantations, in the distinctive weaving of their basket work, their wood carvings, paintings, and colourful jewellery. When I first went out to Sarawak, everything the Dyaks possessed was the creation of their imaginative minds and their own skilful hands.

I once showed a portrait of a Dyak I had painted to a Dyak chief. He held it at every angle; he even lay on his back to see if he could understand it better. Then his natural boastful pride asserted itself.

"I can see that this man is not as I am," he said:"I have a scarlet headcloth and white shell armlets and other ornaments, whereas he has nothing but his tattoo marks upon his arms and buttocks. See how ugly his eyes are and how wretched are his teeth. His hair is thin and badly cut and he has not a fringe as I have. He is a miserable specimen and so is your picture. You should have painted me."

Another time I took an aged Dyak to see a picture that I had made of him. He was thin and his ribs showed in a wonderful pattern beneath his wrinkled skin. He gazed for a long time at the picture and then with an expression of extreme solemnity he shook his head and sadly said, "*Tuak-K'rus. S'rupa anak mati.*" Which means, "Old and thin. I am like the son of the dead."

I went into a fort once where a hundred heads lay waiting to be reclaimed by their relations after the Sarawak Government had successfully put down head-hunting as part of the Dyak's daily life. The amazing part of it was that these people could recognize the heads of their relatives in the smoked and blackened skulls.

They would point at some head, perhaps buried beneath ten or twenty others, and say, "That was once my brother." When I visited them it was considered a great honour for me to have three of those heads hanging over my chair!

The Dyaks were at one time the fiercest of all the Bornean tribes; and it stands to the credit of the administration of three generations of Brookes that these turbulent people have now given up their ancient and violent customs.

When a young Dyak came of age, no matter how handsome he might be, the girls of his tribe thought little of him until he had at least two or three heads to his credit. He could sing his love songs and dance his war dances, but always would come the question, "How many heads hast thou taken?" If he could produce no gruesome trophies the girl would turn on him and say, "Coward! Do not dare to sue my favours unless with a dried head for me to nurse when thou art absent from me, that I may be constantly reminded of thy prowess." So the boy would go hunting as the only means of winning her love.

When he returned with his trophy, preparations would be made for a great feast – the Feast of the Dried Heads. Everyone would contribute his quota of rice, sugar, fruit, fish, wild pig, and cane, and last but by no means least, an intoxicating drink called "tuak" or rice beer. The young girls would be dressed in gala costumes of brass corsets, short coats and beads. The boy who had taken his first head, and thus become a warrior, would be held in the arms of his beloved as she poured the tuak down his throat. The head that he had taken would be displayed on the main veranda of the long-house for all to see the fulfilment of his manhood.

It was a delicate task to teach these people that to sever an old woman's head as she worked in a rice field, just to please the girl you love, is not really a sign of courage or of honour; to have stamped carelessly on their traditions might easily have led to bloodshed and war.

Vyner and I loved these people. They were gay and light-hearted and mischievous as children. They were friendly and warm and loved companionship. After I had been talking to them for a

while they would say, "Since we have spoken our hearts have expanded to the size of the largest fruits upon the most fertile trees."

In strong contrast to the Dyaks in Sarawak were the Malays,
with their delicate and tranquil beauty; an unambitious race, content as long as they had their rice, their sweet drinks, and as many
wives as they could afford. Most of their troubles came from
domestic quarrels, an old wife generally refusing to give way to
a young one. Nothing is actually given to a Malay bride, the
jewellery and clothes are only lent to her so that they can be handed
on to the next one – sometimes with an ill grace. The Malays have
not much use for women except as wives and mothers. Often
when I visited them they would press their hands against my stomach and say, "*Tid'ada anak?*" ("No baby?"). Always I had to
shake my head and say, "No, no babies any more." They had
this touching directness about sexual matters, and, according to
Vyner, they had developed a technique for prolonging intercourse for anything up to three days and nights. I can't imagine
how he knew!

The Malays, the Dyaks, and the Kyans believed my husband
sat side by side with God. They often asked me what he and God
discussed during the day, and if God had a beard or was clean-
shaven like their Rajah. At any official function my husband
walked beneath the royal yellow umbrella, just he alone. I never
sat next to God; and I never walked in the shade of that yellow
umbrella.

On Monday 22 July 1918, Vyner Brooke took the Oath of Accession before the Council Negri and was publicly installed as
Third White Rajah of Sarawak. It was an unforgettable day, for
many reasons, and also the longest that I can ever remember. Nobody who saw Vyner that day realized the difficulties Adeh and I
had been through to get him there at all. He was so jittery that at
one point he even suggested that I should attend the ceremony
alone, and explain to his people that he had been suddenly taken
ill. The uniform that I had designed for him, and all its trimmings,
were laid out on his bed, while I followed him about from room
to room, thrusting brandies into his hand. Outside, in the Astana

garden, the troops were lined up, and the grass slopes were packed
with Malay chiefs, Chinese towkays, Dyak warriors, and Government officers; the Kuching river was a mass of brightly decorated
boats each filled with his loyal subjects. Adeh and I pleaded with
him not to fail his people. His Malay boy held up his uniform and
with tears in his eyes begged him to get dressed. At last with a
shrug of his shoulders he submitted.

Then we discovered that moths and silverfish had found their
way into the gold braided coat, and when he put his arms into the
sleeves there was a sickening rending sound. Hurriedly, we tacked
them on again; there, at last, he stood, perfectly turned out and
looking magnificent in his black uniform with golden palm
leaves down the front of it and round the cuffs; and across his
chest, the ribbon of the G.C.M.G. I did not wear Malay costume
for this ceremony, but a pale pink frock, and a matching picture
hat. I think it was the first and last time I ever wore a hat in
Sarawak.

The river opposite the Astana was transformed. A crimson
banner supported by two tall masts covered with heraldic shields
and miniature flags, spanned the road at the stone landing place.
There was a long triumphal archway hung with garlands of
coloured paper roses and reaching as far as the Court House.

At nine o'clock we came out of the Astana, followed by the
Tuan Muda bearing the Sword of State upon a yellow cushion.
We were taken across the river by the State Barge that had been
a gift from the late King of Siam. We were received at the stone
landing place by the Members of the Supreme Council, and when
we reached the top step the band struck up the Sarawak National
Anthem. We moved slowly forward, the Rajah as usual a little
in advance of me and sheltered by his official royal umbrella. The
Members of the Supreme Council fell into line behind us, with
the Tuan Muda and all the native chiefs, the speed of our progress
down that sunlit path being adjusted to match the great age and
failing strength of one of our most beloved Malay chiefs, the
Datu Bandar.

The interior of the Court House had been transformed into

unimaginable magnificence. At ordinary times, when the cases were tried and my husband sat in solemn judgment, it was gloomy and severe; but now the walls and joists blazed with varied flags and emblems, and the narrow twisted corridors were carpeted in crimson. From the entrance to the dais it was lined on either side by Dyak and Kayan warriors standing shoulder to shoulder, their naked bodies as motionless as images in bronze. Above the dais was a golden canopy over the two decorated chairs which were to be our thrones. As we took our seats, the full beauty of the scene seemed to catch in my throat. The gorgeous native costumes, the uniforms, and the white feathers of the Dyak warriors, stood out from among the thousands of waiting people. Here and there I could pick out a Malay Datu, a Haji fresh from Mecca, a Kayan chieftain with a mighty spear in his hands; and beyond them, a throng of white-clad Chinese with paper flowers in their buttonholes. The so-called savage Dyaks, with their waving plumes of war and their barbaric shields covered with tufts of hair taken from the heads of those they had murdered, and blue tattooing on their perfect bodies, now stood with smiling faces, coloured beads glittering round their necks, looking as if butter would not melt in their mouths.

On the platform were assembled the members of the Council Negri, the Sarawak Government Officers and their wives, and all the European guests. As soon as they were seated, Inchi Abu Bakar proceeded to read aloud the Proclamation announcing the accession of Charles Vyner Brooke, and expounding the meaning of the ceremony that was to follow. When this was over the aged Datu Bandar advanced to the dais and, in an amazingly strong voice, dedicated the Sword of State, which was the symbol of the Raj, to the keeping of the Rajah in the name of the people of the country. Datu Bandar then received the Sword from the Datu Tomonggong, who had held it during the dedication, and, mounting the lower step of the dais, stretched out his arms across the golden cushion bearing the Sword. My husband then rose to his feet, and laying his hand upon the Sword announced in a few ringing words his acceptance of the charge. The Datus retired backwards for a few steps, the Datu Bandar placing the Sword on a pedestal in front of the dais so that all might see it. Then, joining his hands before his face, he pronounced the "Somlah", or fealty, with his head bowed towards the Rajah. All the people throughout the Court House and in the street followed him in gesture and in utterance so that it became like a soft chant over the crowd.

As soon as this died down there came a mighty European cheer; and after the cheer, the Dyaks raised their spears and gave one long triumphant war-cry that echoed as far as the river's edge and was taken up by the people in every small boat and in every narrow street of the Bazaar. During this uproar the two venerable figures of the Datu Bandar and the Datu Tomonggong retired with gentle dignity to their places; their part in the ceremony was at an end. Vyner then descended from the dais and took the Oath of Accession in Malay; the Sarawak National Anthem was played, and there was a thundering salute from the Fort guns. Charles Vyner Brooke was now, in deed and in name, Third White Rajah of Sarawak.

17 Sarawak sights and sounds

M Y HUSBAND began his reign not so much as a
king over his people, but as a shepherd over his
flock. He was their friend and counsellor; their
examiner, and sometimes, much to his regret, their executioner.
For, in the last resort, the Rajah held in his hands the power of life
and death. To a kind and humane man, this was a most terrible
ordeal; to have to look into the frightened eyes of a young Malay
or Dyak murderer, who had perhaps at one time been his friend,
and pronounce the sentence of death upon him. Vyner was above
all else a fair and merciful man, and he had just two answers to
murder. If a man killed his wife's lover he condemned him to a
long term of imprisonment, but if a man murdered merely for
money he condemned him to death. He selected his Government
officers with the utmost care, young men of integrity and understanding from all walks of life. If ever any one of them was heard
to refer to the natives as "bloody niggers" he was out of the
country as quickly as a pellet from a gun.

Vyner was, at that time, a far handsomer man than when I had
first met him. He still had the fair unruly eyebrows, which stood
out from the deep tan of his face; but there was white in his hair
now, and this accentuated the blueness of his eyes. Since his accession to the throne he had acquired a new assurance. He still had
his obstinate chin and sensitive mouth, and, thank God, his sense

of humour; but his shyness never left him, even at home. He was easy to talk to, but not intimate. I had been closer to him than anyone, and yet I realized that I knew practically nothing about him. He was a man who immediately drew attention as soon as he entered a room; and although he preferred to be left alone, he did not like to go unnoticed. He hugged his corner where he would sit and read and send up clouds of smoke from his cigar. He was always "The Rajah"; and I do not remember anyone, apart from his own family and mine, who ever called him by his Christian name.

He knew every chief of every tribe by name. He never forgot a face; and when any of them visited him at the Astana, there was no hesitation when he greeted them. For this they respected him and took him to their hearts.

At first I did not find it easy to accept some of their strange customs and more fashionable deformities – the blackening of their teeth by rubbing in burnt coconut shell pounded up with oil (to prevent them, they said, from looking like dogs); the chewing of betel nut that made their mouths blood-red; the extension of their ear lobes by weighing them down with copper or brass rings; and the way they plucked all the hair from their eyebrows and eyelashes. I wore the Malay costume as simply and unobtrusively as I could until I faded completely into my Oriental background.

Very soon after the Coronation Vyner took me for the first time deep into the interior, and, for the first time, I began to comprehend the full beauty of that amazing country. I went into temples and heard the Koran being read. I sat upon the ground and watched the Seiks beating their drums and losing their identities in ecstasy at the music to their gods. I crept barefooted into the women's quarters of a mosque and squatted amongst them, unconsciously swaying my body to their mysterious chant. I saw the Tamils carrying their images through the streets of the bazaar in an orgy of hysterical delight; and witnessed the most wonderful ceremony of all, the Chinese Wankang, or Chasing Out of Devils.

The procession was gay with banners and decorated canopies, and was led by bands of musicians and long files of fantastically dressed youths seated upon all kinds of artificial animals. Then came triumphal cars loaded with paper flowers, upon which rode bejewelled "maidens" who were in reality boys posing in graceful attitudes. As they were borne along, water was raised to them on poles to moisten their parched lips. A huge paper dragon with crimson jaws wide open wound its tortuous way through the procession, constantly snapping at an immense and tantalizing golden orb that hung just out of reach. Each object in the long display had its own legendary significance.

The essential parts of the ceremony were the Chai-lians and the Mystic Junk. The Chai-lians, who were handsome youths of between ten and eighteen years of age, bore with them purple banners, and their standard-bearer was the tallest and most muscular Chinese I had ever seen. On either side of him walked his assistants, beating drums. The Chai-lians were dressed in richly embroidered tunics and purple trousers, with head-dresses that were strangely and profusely decorated, and made to taper in a forward curve after the fashion of a Punchinello. They marched in single file singing an incantation invoking the GREAT ONE to bring peace and plenty to Sarawak. The faces of these boys were highly coloured and their full lips were painted like scarlet canna petals. They had perfectly arched eyebrows over their narrow eyes, like crescent moons. They were expressionless as images, and it was difficult to realize that they were flesh and blood.

In the Mystic Junk there was almost everything that the entrapped spirits were likely to require on that long journey from which they would never return; rice, firewood, salt, sugar, various vegetables, one live pig, two fowls – one cooked and the other crowing dismally to be set free. There were three sets of sacred weapons from the temple, eight wooden cannons, five silk umbrellas, fourteen shields, a cooking set, flags and fans, and a case full of carpenter's tools. In the three cabins there were small model bedsteads with pillows and mosquito nets, and there was a paper captain with his paper crew.

The Wankang proceeded to the spot selected for the burning of the junk. It was followed by hundreds of spectators who neither walked nor ran, but who swayed in an uncanny kind of dance, accompanied by a weird and melancholy instrument, and by the beating of gongs and drums. Carts and rickshaws followed, loaded with fuel for the kindling of the junk; and as the great ship appeared, the crowds, who were lined up on either side of the road with joss sticks in their hands, fell down on their knees and offered obeisance.

The junk itself was a masterpiece. I could hardly believe that the angry figures sitting at bow and stern were really only made of paper. Their expressions were vivid and real and grotesquely alive. Enormous white tusks protruded from the corners of their mouths with blood-red gums and long gold tentacles. The junk itself was perfect with its three tall masts and pure white sails like quivering ghostly wings. We stood round in a wide circle as the fuel was placed beneath it; then, at a given signal, everyone hurled their lighted joss sticks against the ship. Spellbound, we watched the sparks turn into a blaze and the blaze into high roaring flames. All through those many minutes, while the paper junk was burning and its magnificence turning to ashes, not one word was spoken.

The crowd stood in absolute silence, with the smoke curling in grey wreaths around their heads. When the last little flag was crumpled by the flames and the whole thing lay upon the water, charred and broken, a sigh went through the company of people – the rustling of the devils as they started on their journey. It was a moment of intense drama; and, for me, of alienation. In the yellow masks and slanting eyes around me was a wisdom and a meaning that would be for ever beyond my reach.

I knew this, and yet already the Far East had laid its spell on me, and I greatly loved the different races and people who lived in Sarawak. In addition, my Rajah had given me a name, three beautiful daughters, and as much of his heart as he could offer. He had made me a part of a unique history and given me the anchorage I had always longed for, and turned me from a dull and simple girl into a woman.

18   Wives and Dyaks

With the Great War still raging and its out-come still in doubt, we returned to England and our house on Wimbledon Common. Four months later the Germans were in full retreat, and were soon suing for an armistice.

It was not easy to settle down to a normal life after four years of war; and if it had not been for Vyner with his light-hearted philosophy, I would still have gone on watching the sky and listening for sirens. We moved from Wimbledon to London, to a house in Airlie Gardens, Campden Hill, almost next door to where Leonora had been born.

We were very happy there and the children were able to go to a little day school at Notting Hill; but I knew it would not be for long. After living in Sarawak, we were always restless in England, and in twenty-five years we had fifteen different houses, but never a permanent home. Some of them Vyner never even went into. He just rented them for me and the children and then returned to Sarawak.

It was at Airlie Gardens that my husband suddenly decided that he would learn to dance. If he had told me he was going to swim the Channel, I could not have been more surprised. We went to the Empress Rooms in Knightsbridge, because we were told it was the right place to go; and it was there that Vyner first began to indulge, in real earnest, his delight in "les girls" that lasted for the whole of his life.

It started with the one we nicknamed "the woeful giraffe". As we were standing watching the instructors and instructresses whirling round with their inexpert and awkward pupils, I noticed a tall slim girl with a sad and pensive expression, and long thick lashes that drooped over melancholy eyes. I turned to point her out to Vyner, but the wicked look in his eye told me that he had already seen her.

"I think I'd like that one to teach me, Mip," he said, "if you could arrange it?"

If I could! He knew perfectly well that if he had asked me to find the Venus of Milo to instruct him, I would have produced the next best thing. That was the way I was with him, from the time we married until the end. I therefore arranged that the Woeful Giraffe should be Vyner's instructress; and I selected for myself a charming and kindly man, who was a marvellous dancer and who later became the famous band leader, Victor Sylvester.

The Woeful Giraffe was called Toby Johns, and nature had provided her with large blue eyes, and a face that was pretty, yet not "pretty". Vyner dragged her with him everywhere. Wherever they went I was obliged to go too. "It looks better," Vyner insisted, "that I should be out with my wife." But the sort of relationship that those two had *could* only look one way, whether I was with them or not.

Then quite suddenly Vyner became bored. That was his way, with houses and things and people. He drove them hard and then lost interest. I went home one evening and found our drawing-room hung with wreaths. To each wreath he had attached a card – his night-club membership cards. On a placard stretched across the room he had written: "Farewell to Night Life in London". It was the burial of his dancing days – though not of Toby Johns, who remained one of our greatest friends until, at a very early age, she died.

On account of our children I had been obliged to return to England every year; but when Valerie was four years old, I decided to take them all out to Sarawak. It seemed that our life out there as a united family would be better than the constant partings, tears, and separations. It may have upset the conventional pattern of their lives, but it gave them a richness of sympathy and friendship towards the Sarawak people that they never forgot.

Our days in Sarawak followed a definite routine. We woke at 6 a.m. and went from our bedrooms to the coolness of the veranda where we drank tea and ate mango and pawpaw. We gloried in the sun rising slowly through a soft grey mist, and the little town emerging gay and colourful from its cloak of night. Cocks would begin to crow, and the cries of the Chinese water-carriers would herald the dawning of the day. At 7 a.m. we were served with the rest of our breakfast, still on the cool veranda. During the early morning Vyner and I went about our special occupations; I to my writing and painting, and he to his law chair and books. Like his father, he wasn't one for comfort, and sat in a canvas deck-chair, which was usually torn. At eight o'clock he would cross the river to the Court House. When the Court was in session he would be accompanied by his official guard, and would walk beneath the yellow umbrella carrying a walking-stick with a heavily embossed silver handle which was the emblem of his office.

After he had left I would often relax in the swimming pool with a gin sling, or go shopping in the bazaar, or visit some friends. At noon a cannon boomed and Vyner would return to the Astana. We would have a few drinks before lunch; and then as soon as we had finished, it was siesta time; at least for me, if not for Vyner. Back he would go to his old deck-chair, his cigar, and his books.

At 3.30 p.m. we kept a kind of open court when the Malays, Dyaks, and Chinese were welcome visitors at the Astana. There were no formalities or presentations; they just came and went as they wished. Vyner received the men in one group while I, in my limited Malay, endeavoured to entertain the women. The talk would mostly be about the grievances and problems of their homes, the men complaining about their shrewish jealous wives, and the women about the meanness of their husbands. What they were usually after was a small loan to buy or repair a house, or to purchase a sarong, bracelet, or brooch. At four-thirty these interviews would end, and we were free to cross the river to play golf or tennis, or go for a drive along our one road. Then we would go to the Club for billiards or Mah Jong and drinks.

On Saturday evenings Vyner held a roulette game, for women only; and every Sunday we had a swimming party with gin slings and an enormous curry. There was not much outside entertainment in Sarawak. and we had to do the best we could with the materials to hand. But we had fun.

I soon discovered that, in this limited Government society, my safest course was to be all things to all men. I had to learn to ignore malicious gossip, try and avoid prejudice, and treat all people honestly and fairly. It was not always easy. We both tried to be impartial to our Government officers and their wives, but it was only natural that we should like some more than others. They, of course, had their own interests at heart, and many of the wives were pretty and alluring. Vyner was kind, just, and benevolent, but his weakness was women. They knew this well enough, and used it if they could. In a sense, I had the same problem with the men, who were ready enough with their attentions and flattery to try and advance themselves with Vyner through me. Such temptations are inevitable for people who had, as we did, absolute power. Though we were both vigilant and watchful we were sometimes fooled.

I suppose I became more vulnerable and human in Sarawak than I had ever been before. You must remember my rigid upbringing, and the fact that when I married at twenty-four I knew nothing of men, if you except the bungled explorations of my father's shameless secretary. I was curious; I think I actually wanted to be made love to; and it was all too easy for me to encourage our Government officers to believe that if they addressed their attentions to me, I would influence Vyner to promote them.

Both he and I had embittering experiences, never knowing whether or not we were merely the targets for place-seekers and adventurers. Luckily for both of us, our marriage was securely based on friendship. I have never really known the meaning of

passionate love; only the loyal and gentle attention of an undemonstrative man. If I ever tried to tell Vyner that I was sorry
or ashamed of anything I had done, he would say, "Nonsense,
Mip, you are my wife."

There were times when I felt very insecure, not because people
were unkind to me, but because they were unused to a woman
being thrust into the foreground. Malay wives did not speak unless they were spoken to, nor did they raise their eyes from their
folded hands. I endeavoured in my faltering Malay to draw them
out, but they continued to sit still and silent, so that the distance
between us seemed at times impenetrable. Slowly I improved my
knowledge of the language, and whenever I went shopping there
was a constant murmur following me through the kampong. The
children would gather round the doorways whispering and giggling when I stopped; little girls behind coloured veils who would
become women too soon, and mothers at the age of twelve.
Whilst our children were romping and playing with their toys,
these sedately powdered and perfumed little girls were being given
away in marriage to men often three times their age. Fruit ripened
quickly beneath the tropical sun, and was plucked early from the
trees; but these child wives did not mind. They were proud of
their decorated marriage bed, and glad to humour an elderly husband. For several nights after they were married, an older woman
would sleep between them, and instruct the little twelve-year-old
in the various enticements of sexual relationship, passing on to her
her knowledge of voluptuous skills.

A barren wife was a shameful thing in any Malay family, and
the child wife would already have had a lover or two; for Sarawak
was a land of uncensored free love and there was very little violence or rape. When these little girls married they possessed their
husbands; and beneath their downcast eyes there was the fire and
fury and the jealousy of ownership. If their husbands were invited
to a party without them they would climb into the trees outside
the house where it was being held, and the glistening whites of
their eyes would look like little fireflies. If a man was too attentive
to one of the female guests, he would be beaten with his wife's

VYNER BROOKE, THE RAJAH MUDA,
1912 AND THE RANEE MUDA IN
SARAWAK COSTUME
(shortly after her marriage)

THE RAJAH AND HIS FAMILY
(*left to right*, Leonora, the Ranee, Valerie, the Rajah, a
Elizabeth)

THE RAJAH AND HIS SARAWAK RANGERS IN FRONT OF THE ASTANA

THE RANEE: FIRST WOMAN OF SARAWAK TO FLY

LEONORA BROOKE AND THE EARL OF
INCHCAPE

'TEA AT THE ASTANA'
(*left to right*, Gerald MacBryan, the Tuan Muda,
the Ranee, the Rajah)

ELIZABETH
BROOKE

belt when he returned home, and his life would become a torment of revenge. This particularly applied to the Government officers whose mistresses were determined to keep their men at any cost.

After I had been in Sarawak for a while I began to make many friends among the people. I remember three in particular. One was a Chinese called Wee Khen Chiang, a brilliant and ambitious man with the lined face of one who has had to work hard for everything. He amassed great riches, became very powerful, and eventually owned vast properties and a bank. I called him "The Uncrowned King of Sarawak", and often told him he was a rascal and a rogue, and this delighted him so much that he would send for a bottle of champagne and drink to it. Many people both feared and hated him, and his life was threatened. However, he survived, and during the Japanese occupation of Sarawak in World War II risked his life to supply cigarettes to the Government officers in the Kuching concentration camp. He would creep out at night and push the precious packets through the prison bars when the guards were not looking. A brave act from a Chinese towards the British captives.

My two other friends were Dyaks; one a famous warrior called Koh. He was of medium height, well built and with amazing muscles in his arms and legs. He was heavily tattooed, and wore boar's tusks through his ears; an assortment of bracelets and neck-laces, and a scarlet "chawat" or loin cloth. Sometimes he would wear a great war jacket made from goat skins. He could be haughty and overbearing, but there was something immensely engaging and attractive about him, particularly when he recited his legends in a high sing-song voice.

He told me that the reason his people had no literature was that the Creator, having given a language to mankind, had assembled the oldest man from each nation in order to communicate to them the use of letters. All of them received these written signs, but the man from Borneo swallowed his, so that they were united with his body and changed into memory. Thereafter their history, their laws and their agreements were printed in their hearts as surely as if they had been written down, and every Dyak knew the legends of his gods and of his tribe. All this he would tell me in faltering Malay and faultless Dyak – not a word of which I could understand without Vyner by my side. Then he would dance; and the natural grace and beauty, the ecstasy in his half-closed eyes, contained a whole alien world.

My other friend was called Tedong, which means "snake", because of his noiseless movements through the tangled jungle. He was perhaps the most beautiful Dyak boy I ever saw. When I first met him he was too young to be a warrior, his ears were unpierced by boar's tusks and he wore few ornaments. He knew he was handsome, and he would sit on our veranda while one of his sisters combed the thick black hair that reached as far as his waist. Tedong did not shave his eyebrows, pluck out his eyelashes, blacken his teeth, or in any other way disfigure his magnificent good looks. His eyes were brown and deep as the jungle pools, and he had the arched eyebrows of a Botticelli angel. I sometimes wondered whether he was in fact pure Dyak, or perhaps the out-come of some encounter between East and West.

The Dyaks ravished my senses, the boys as much as the young girls, who, with uplifted naked breasts, were simple and un-ashamed, and had delicate swift movements like little wild fauns. Head-hunters they may have been; but who could feel afraid of these pale brown warriors with their moments of great gentleness, their laughter, their strange customs, legends, and primitive beliefs? All I felt was amazement and fascination.

Cables from England were urging me to return, and I could not decide what I ought to do. I knew that Vyner depended on me to help him fight his loneliness in the long, white-walled Ast-ana; and although I convinced myself he would never leave me, I was well aware of the dangers. Women formed the clouds that menaced my marriage for fifty-four years. I was never jealous, but I was mortally afraid.

Apart from the Government officers' wives, I found my hus-band kept a variety of other pets. There was an unsociable but apparently harmless boa-constrictor which lived up in the roof of the Astana, and which would come slithering down into the garden as soon as the sun rose. There was also a tame porcupine which used to frequent my bathroom. It took a violent dislike to me and would throw its quills at me as soon as I descended the steps, so that I was obliged to go down to my shower with an open umbrella in front of me. Vyner also had five or six monkeys of all sizes which followed him round the garden like dogs. The only way he could catch them was to make me walk in front of him. They would then spring straight at me and he would grab them on the way. Monkeys are very seldom friendly with women unless they are kept in captivity; and there were only two that really liked me, twin baby orang-utans whom I named Gin and Bitters. I took them everywhere, carrying one on each arm; and they would lift up their large leathery faces to be kissed. They had a passion for ice cream. Vyner gave Gin to the Prince of Wales, now Duke of Windsor, when he visited Sarawak; and poor Bitters died of a broken heart.

19 *Lepers and crocodiles*

HEN WE RETURNED to England we kept changing houses like uneasy birds who cannot settle. We even went back to "Orchard Lea" for a time; but one should never retrace one's footsteps. The children were happy there, but Vyner and I never felt the house was really ours. At any moment round any corner I thought I might meet the two little boys whose boots I had been obliged to button, or my fair-haired sister who was so unafraid of all the things that I feared. "Orchard Lea" was too full of memories altogether.

We moved to London, and took a regal-looking house in Portland Place. I now began to entertain, though only when Vyner was in Sarawak. I started giving Bohemian parties, Chinese suppers and unconventional At Homes, and was described in the papers as "one of the best-dressed women in Society" – I, who had once had my cuffs fastened with safety pins and holes in my stockings!

The children were now growing up. Their friends filled our home and came and went in an endless stream. Life seemed so much easier for Noni, Didi, and Vava than it had been for me. They never had to stand in a row of anxious virgins as I had done, waiting to be asked to dine or dance. They had beauty, and a certain notoriety, for their Sarawak background made them ready-made material for the gossip columns. Everything "The Three Princesses" did was exaggerated and glamourized.

On 2 December 1930, my father died. My mother telephoned and asked me to go round to her in Tilney Street. She said that one moment he was talking and laughing; and then he had gone into his dressing-room on the ground floor and dropped dead behind the door. She was not certain he was dead; he might be asleep. She wanted me to go in and make sure.

I had never seen anyone dead before. I touched his hands, and they were still soft and warm. He looked young, the lines gone from his face, and peaceful. I remember thinking to myself, "You will never be able to hurt me any more." I had no feeling of loss or sorrow because I had never really loved him. I remembered him saying once, "As one grows older nobody cares whether one is on the earth or under it."

Very soon after this, Vyner and I returned to Sarawak, and I found myself involved in a round of minor official duties, attending school sports, mission schools, hospitals, and so forth. I remember there was one man I used to visit who shed his skin every year like a snake. First he would start to shiver, and then there would be a weird rustling sound as his skin slowly peeled from his entire body. The flesh beneath was very red and tender to touch. None of the doctors could explain this strange phenomenon. The man himself was rather cross at the interest we took in him.

Then Vyner asked me to visit the Leper Camp. A surge of horror and fear came over me, and I had to fight desperately with my revulsion. He did not insist, but I felt how much he wanted me to go, and finally I agreed.

There were three hundred and eighty-four lepers in that camp, which lay thirteen miles along the Ponnisoin road outside Kuching. Two hundred and ninety-one were men, eighty women and thirteen children. The eldest child was twelve, the youngest four. When I saw them, my fear turned to pity and an intense desire to do everything I could for them.

The Camp was divided into three, one part for each race. Everything was kept as much like an ordinary village as possible, and apart from a Dispensary where they went for their injections and the dressing of their sores, the Dyaks, Malays, and Chinese lived as they were accustomed to. A rota of work amongst the able-bodied men enabled them to earn about twenty cents a day. Dyaks and Chinese who had saved a little managed to keep pigs, and these pigs were bought by the Government for consumption in the settlement. The lepers cut their own firewood and sold it to those unfit for such work, and they in their turn would keep a few chickens or grow vegetables.

The Government provided essential rations. Few people outside ever thought of the lepers; visits from relatives were rare, and the only clothes they ever received were oddments issued from the Police Department. There were no recreations for them in the evenings until I presented them with a gramophone and several hundred records. One of the dressers would play it outside the makeshift Dispensary, and everyone would squat round and listen to it in rapt attention.

I found that deep in the heart of most of them was the hope that one day they would be cured, and able to return to their homes. But nobody, not even their own families, wanted to have anything to do with a discharged leper. They were afraid of his disfigurement, ashamed of his handless arms and footless legs. It is terrible to realize that there are still many people like these spending year after year in a living death.

Having once overcome my fear, I went regularly to see them, taking them blankets, costume jewellery, and toys. I would wear long canvas boots tied tightly above my knees, and the doctor would wash my arms and hands with strong disinfectant so that I could move safely among the pitiful collection of helpless and unhappy souls.

While in Sarawak this time I published another book. It was called *The Cauldron*, and was a collection of macabre short stories with an Eastern background, many of them based on fact. The critics commended them for their "power and characterization"; one even went so far as to say, "In 'The Cauldron' we have a book of short stories that convey not a little of the emotion that is experienced at the first reading of 'Macbeth'. It is a brilliant book."

My next book was a novel, called *Lost Property*. It told of the loves of a brother and sister, children of a British father and a Malay mother, who lived in a little country village and then moved to London. This book was cautiously but well received, and was described as being ahead of its time; the problems of half-castes and Eurasians and the tragedy of their lost and twilit world meant little to those who had not seen them at first hand.

Quite suddenly my brother Maurice died. He had been out shooting on the Callander moors, and had complained of feeling tired and had gone to rest in his room. Three or four hours later, my mother went upstairs and found he had died in his sleep. His wife, Zena Dare, was in a play with Ivor Novello at the time, and had to go through the ordeal of acting before an audience which knew of her bereavement, and sympathized by the warmth of their applause.

When we returned to England I started giving my Bohemian parties again. I was described in the newspapers as one of the most beautiful, accomplished, and popular hostesses in London, and the most charming of despots. But when I looked in the mirror, all I saw was the reflection of a frightened little girl who had once planned to kill herself.

In the first few years of his reign my husband took things easily. Whereas the old Rajah had never gone about unarmed, Vyner moved among his people with nothing more formidable than a camera. He went into the interior to make peace among the Dyaks with the help of my friend Pengula Koh, who at that time was the head of the Dyaks in the Rejang river. A group of rebels had formed under a Dyak called Asun. He was a dangerous character; but eventually he gave himself up and was banished to Lundu, the remote outstation where the old Rajah had begun his service, and where we sent our troublemakers.

One of the first big changes that Vyner made was to disband the Sarawak Rangers and turn them into a constabulary force. It was all part of his policy of gradual modernization with as little disturbance as possible of traditional customs. And so Sarawak gradually changed while we watched. The value of land increased; and Vyner encouraged his people not to rely entirely upon rubber, but to grow rice on part of their land. It seemed absurd that Sarawak could not produce enough rice to be self-supporting; but people were more interested in the profits to be culled from rubber, and the increasing output of the Miri oilfields.

It was at this time that I went on my first and last crocodile hunt. Some of our rivers were infested by crocodiles, and many Malays had been flicked out of their small boats and devoured.

I went with a Dyak called Ubi, whose father and grandfather had all been crocodile trappers. Ubi's real name was Turan which in Dyak means "Shining Light", but when he became a man they changed his name in the way that his tribe have, and called him Ubi which means "Potato". I asked him if he minded this indignity, and he grinned and replied that changing a name did not alter a man. In his own mind he was still Turan.

Ubi was supposed to be possessed with supernatural power over crocodiles, and he maintained that it was easier than catching crabs. He was of middle height, muscular, and beautifully formed except for his legs which were slightly bent from squatting on his Takai Buriet or seat-mat, which hung behind him from his belt. His skin was tanned a deep brown, and his black hair fringed his forehead and hung down to his waist. Most of the time he chewed betel nut and spat scarlet saliva over the side of the boat. He knew about as little Malay as I did, so conversation was limited and abrupt. I already knew that he had lost his wife. She had been seized by a crocodile in front of his eyes while washing herself in the river, and it was this one that Ubi was out to capture.

We started late in the afternoon as we had not far to travel. I wore an old shirt with long sleeves and my high canvas boots to protect me from the sandflies and mosquitoes. Our boat seemed inadequate and dangerously small. In the bows sat Ubi paddling vigorously, while I sat in the middle, clutching the sides. Behind me was Ubi's younger brother with the tackle, harpoon, and a lantern.

The blue of the sky began to pale and the sun turned crimson as it sank towards the horizon. When it reached the edge of the river it would be dark. Along the mud banks we could just see the young crocodiles stirring like logs of wood and slipping from the mud into the river. We turned into a small tributary stream where the water moved slowly through the mangrove swamps. Suddenly the sun was gone, and night was upon us like a blanket. Ubi's brother lit the lantern and held it up on the end of a pole. Ubi watched the water with a fierce intensity, as if he would draw the crocodile from the bottom of the river with his eyes. "It will soon be over, Tuan Ranee," he said. When I asked him how he knew, he replied that a certain bird had just whistled, and this he took to be a good omen.

We were in a deep pool by now, and Ubi took hold of the harpoon. This consisted of a heavy metal head with a socket into which a long pole was loosely inserted. A line, made of rattan, was attached to the head.

Ubi continued to stare, motionless, at the black water, and I felt my hair beginning to lift off my scalp. Then we saw our prey, an immense crocodile, floating near us, its head lying on the water and the rest of its body hanging almost at right angles. Its eyeballs showed up clearly in the reflection from our lantern, like two flames floating on the surface of the stream.

Ubi stood poised, the harpoon grasped in his hands. Then with a mighty thrust he drove the point into the back of its neck. This is the brute's most vunerable spot, where the skin is unprotected by "buttons". Ubi pulled out the harpoon's shaft and waited, the rattan line in his hand. The crocodile sank to the bottom, and then began to fight.

Immediately the pool was churned into a maelstrom, and the boat rocked and pitched as Ubi calmly "played" the crocodile, as one plays a fish. I clung to the canoe's sides for dear life, and wished desperately that I had not come. And then, quite suddenly, the battle was over; the fifteen foot man-eating crocodile was beaten. Ubi handed the line to his brother and quietly paddled us back to the Astana, with the crocodile being towed astern.

There was a great crowd standing waiting by the Astana steps, and I could just see Vyner's figure leaning over the veranda rail. The crocodile was dragged ashore, and Ubi began to hack at its underparts. His birds of omen had told him that this was the brute that had seized his sixteen-year-old wife and dragged her screaming into the river; now he would find out the truth. Suddenly, with a great shout, he drew from the reptile's belly three gold bracelets, a little gold chain on which hung a tiny crucifix, and a roll of dark hair. He dipped the bracelets in the river to wash off the blood, and peered at them closely, "It is written here," he whispered, "'Empari'. That was my wife's name." He did not cry, because Dyaks seldom weep; but slowly the tormented look went out of his face, and he said very simply, "Although my heart is but a shadow I have been avenged and am at peace."

Never was I more thankful to find myself safe within the white walls of the Astana. When I told Vyner that we had caught the crocodile, he looked up for a moment from his book and replied, "Of course you did, Mip; you've got your father's brain." I do not believe he was listening.

20 *Girls and daughters*

THERE CAME OUT to Sarawak at about this time a young man who was destined to play a sinister part in the history of the Sarawak Raj. His name was Gerard MacBryan, and he was the son of a doctor who kept a mental hospital at Box, near Bath. He once told me that, as a child, his father insisted on taking him on his rounds of the hospital and how terrified he had been of some of the incoherent ravings of the patients. I don't know if this experience was responsible, but it was odd, to say the least, that eventually he became insane himself.

Vyner had recruited him, quite unaware that he was anything but a perfectly normal fellow, who had had an unhappy spell in the Navy; but quite soon after he arrived at the small outstation where he was going to work, rumours began to reach us of strange goings-on there. MacBryan, it was said, suffered from hallucinations that his bungalow was being attacked, and would start shooting wildly into the darkness.

Vyner and I were intrigued, and he was summoned to Kuching. I well remember the day he was ushered into the presence of the Rajah. He was only eighteen, tall and unnaturally thin, and he wore an enormous sombrero hat. He was extremely good-looking with a pallid skin and small grey-green eyes that were never still. His greatest charm was his laugh; it shook his whole frame, as if it came welling from some central spring of merriment in him. Vyner had a talk with him; and after he had left he leaned back in his chair and said, "By jove, Mip, what a wonderful fellow; but he's nuts."

Our three daughters were with us in Sarawak, and playing havoc with the emotions of our Government officers. They had all their father's mischievous desire for adoration, and a great deal of my longing for love, without my inhibitions. Vyner looked on with tolerance, because he saw himself in them, and only put his foot down when their affairs interfered with the work of his officers.

As usual, I had plenty to keep me occupied and content. I began to try my hand at drawing in pastels. There were endless subjects all round me in Sarawak; and when the pictures were exhibited at the Walker Galleries in Bond Street, they sold well, and one critic in particular became quite lyrical. "The marvellous colouring," he wrote, "the crimson and gold of the sunset, the vivid beauty of the tropical flowers, the silvery glory of the moonlight across the still river, the quaint, picturesque native huts and the green depths of the palm groves must be seen to be believed."

I wrote a three-act play, called *The Heels of Pleasure*, on my pet theme, the question of Eurasians, which was presented at the Arts Theatre Club on a trial run of a week, but unfortunately went no further. Disappointed but not dismayed, I followed it up with a comedy called *Persecuted Parents* which I hoped might lure Marie Tempest, but without success.

In the meantime my Rajah was misbehaving himself in his own inimitable way. It was a side of his character that I could regard with tolerance, for it was part of his colour and charm. Some people may find this hard to believe, but they did not know my husband. He was a sweetheart in every sense of the word; so kind and good that I could surely allow him one imperfection – his shy but resolute approach to women.

I was completely confident that he would never leave me, because our marriage was based on friendship, tolerance, and devotion. These outside loves of his were his little foolishness, and, at the same time, a form of escape from his diffidence and shyness.

Perhaps the oddest thing about it was that I knew them all; and I would look at the outwardly innocent faces of some of the Government officers' wives and remember what he had told me about them, and about himself. In a way it gave me a feeling of power; because, in spite of them all, he still belonged to me. It is easy enough to dismiss my compliance as resignation, or as the discarding of all semblance of a moral code; but remember it was not entirely Vyner's fault. Although I had thawed considerably in the Sarawak sun, I was still, to all intents and purposes, a frigid woman.

Anyway, as I've said, I knew them all, in Sarawak and in England. I still have some of their love-letters which Vyner would often send on to me. He pretended he wanted me to see how un-initiated and inexperienced they were; but I did not find them so ignorant and green, not by any means. Some of them really loved him, and he knew it, and that wicked man of mine wanted me to know it too. Sometimes he would write to me and say, "Darling Mip, I've found a new girl. I just can't wait until you see her and tell me what you think of her, if you don't like her I will get rid of her at once."

How could I be angry with anyone who was so naive and ingenuous as that? Luckily I liked nearly all his girls and some of them became my greatest friends. During our fifty-two years of married life there were only three I begged him to discard. One was a gold-digger, one a thundering bore, and the other a nymphomaniac.

They came in all shapes and sizes. There was one, I remember, who had a mania for turning somersaults, presumably in order to display her very beautiful legs! There was an opera singer he took to Ascot Races, where she fainted over the rails; and there was one who liked being made love to over the back of a chair. I thought this somewhat unusual, but there is no accounting for tastes.

There was one in Sarawak whom Vyner used to meet in the churchyard. This seemed to me a little irreverent; but he would say, "Where else can I go, Mip, where I'm not followed and spied upon and some damned sentry doesn't pop up from behind a hedge presenting arms?" There was another who lived in a bungalow close to the Astana. My husband's footsteps wore a little path to the bungalow, which, as far as I know, is still there.

There was yet another whom he met on board ship. She had the most lovely madonna-like face, though she was far from being an angel. When the Japanese occupied Sarawak they found some of her letters written to Vyner at the Astana. They were so impressed by their "warmth" that they framed them and hung them on the wall. They were still there when we returned after the war.

The one I liked best of all was a young woman with a cheerful roguish face, who came round to our country house in England, selling flags for some wartime charity, accompanied by her little seven-year-old boy. Vyner was not very fond of children, and the little boy was a constant source of irritation to him. However, I told him, even the Rajah of Sarawak could not have everything his own way.

As he grew older, so his girls became younger. He did not seem to mind their immaturity and baby talk; he said he liked guiding their innocent footsteps into the path of righteousness! Having read some of their letters to him, it seemed to me that in many cases he arrived on the scene too late for that.

When I look back on my life with my incredible husband, I can find no real fault with anything he did. He was not immoral; he was just a man entirely without morals. His girls were of no great importance to him, at any rate in the early years. They simply lent colour to his secluded life and eased his inferiority complex. But the little egotism he had, they fed; and afterwards they became a necessity, a kind of drug. But never during our many years together did he once forget that I was his wife. I was still on the pedestal where he had placed me when he first fell in love with me, a little shaken and a little bent, perhaps, but still there. I was, and remained, Ranee of Sarawak, and none of his women ever succeeded in supplanting me, though many would have liked to.

★   ★   ★   ★

It is difficult to say what impression Vyner's escapades had upon our three young daughters. They had travelled so often out to Sarawak that their outlook and knowledge of life was broad and understanding. Yet I am afraid they were a little shocked by their father's outspokenness; especially Leonora, who idolized him and considered him her personal property. I have often discussed it with them since, and we have laughed about it; but behind their laughter I have detected a trace of bitterness – chiefly, I think, because he was not more attentive to them when they were young.

They had all been born within two years of each other, and they got married in the same order. First Leonora in 1933, then Elizabeth in 1935, and finally Valerie in 1937. Noni first became engaged to a Rumanian Senator called Max Ausnit, who was a majority shareholder in half-a-dozen iron and steel works and Managing Director of the Austrian State Railway Co. of Vienna, and heaven knows what else besides. He gave Noni an engagement ring with a solitaire diamond that looked like the Rock of Gibraltar, which she was too self-conscious to wear. However, it wasn't quite hefty enough to seal the engagement; because on the way home from Sarawak she met and fell in love with the Earl of Inchcape. He was Chairman of P. & O., and a widower with four small children. Noni broke off her engagement, and in due course became the Countess of Inchcape.

Altogether I have had, at one time or another, eight sons-in-law, and a more varied collection would be hard to find. They included, apart from the earl, a band leader, an all-in wrestler, a Spanish fruit importer, a Scottish city business-man, two American colonels and, finally, one Texan.

I have to confess that, at times, I became confused as to who was married to whom and when and where; I also admit that this mosaic of my daughters' marriages has afforded me the utmost interest and amusement. Not so Vyner. He never interfered; but if one of them threatened to visit him he would inform them that they could have fifteen minutes of his time and no more.

The first time I learnt about Didi's wild infatuation for Harry Roy was on one of my return visits from Sarawak. I met him, and could understand where the attraction lay; but Didi did not marry only Harry Roy. In the Jewish manner, she found she had also taken on his mother, his sister, his brother, and his brother-in-law. The women went about in a cloud of mink coats and diamond brooches, all lived next door to one another, all decorated their apartments alike – the Roy syndicate was there to stay. I loved Harry, I admired his genius, his capacity for work, his delightful personality. But I was only his mother-in-law; I did not have to live with him. How can anyone on the outside say what first makes a marriage go wrong? I think part of the trouble was that Harry never belonged to any particular person, not even to his wife and children. He belonged to the public, to the applause and the glare of the footlights; but above all he was dedicated to the Roys.

Now there was only Valerie left; Vava, the natural flirt. From the moment she began to think about anything, she thought about men; and she finally fell face-first for an all-in wrestler by the name of Bob Gregory. There was nothing we could do about it, since she was twenty-two; and they drove all over London in a white open car with "Baba and Bob" painted on the back of it, and with Vava carrying a toy fur monkey, larger than she was, wherever she went.

I became very fond of Bob Gregory; but I was not married to him either. He and Vava went to America; they were living in Los Angeles when, one day, Vava made me a long-distance call. She was ill, could I come? I shall never forget the sight that met my eyes when I opened the door.

It was a small room; and at the back of it stood Bob, doing physical jerks with an enormous crowbar in his hands, completely oblivious to everything else. In the middle of the floor was an overturned metal dish, from which the most extraordinary noise was coming; this turned out to be a baby duckling that Vava was

MUJIK HUNTER

KENYAH HUNTER

SEA DYAK GIRL

SEA DYAK MAN

DYAK GIRLS CARRYING SMOKED HEADS

INTERIOR OF A KAYAN HOUSE

harbouring. The kitchen was stacked with unwashed dishes, and an old Negro stood around muttering and mournfully shaking his head. Vava lay prostrate in a basket chair. Gone were the sunshine and the gaiety; she looked a ghost of her former self.

It was a picture of incompatibility, and was neither's fault. She did not belong to the wrestling world, and he had made the mistake of flourishing the name of Princess Baba, roaring it and blaring it wherever he went. Vava had had bottles thrown at her in Detroit, and had been booed by the tough guys that hang around every Wrestling Club, and who were not impressed with Bob Gregory's 'Princess'. She had something of Vyner's hatred of public exposure, his repugnance to trading on his name; and although poor Bob was only fighting for recognition, the crudity of his methods not only failed, but wrecked his marriage. When the tour was over, Vava left America and never saw Bob again. This was the first of my daughters' various marriages to end.

21 Queen of the Head-Hunters

FOR YEARS I did no writing at all. Then I had the idea of doing a synopsis for a film round the life of James Brooke. I called it "The Great White Rajah", and, without much hope, sent it to Warner Bros. To my profound astonishment they bought an option on it. I thought I was a millionaire. I knew nothing about the motion picture business; and stupidly, instead of consulting a literary agent, I signed a contract which, for a few hundred dollars, gave them the film rights. When Warner Bros. tentatively suggested that I should go to Hollywood and see them, I jumped at the idea.

Before I left, I went to see the Ranee Margaret who had not been feeling well. She was living in a flat off Regent's Park, which was just as dreary as her house had been. But she herself was still beautiful; her eyes, so like my husband's, were still as blue. She was dressed in grey chiffon with a black velvet ribbon round her throat and a little chiffon scarf upon her head. I noticed how quiet and erect she was, with her gloved hands resting in her lap, those marvellous hands that she still preserved to play her eternal piano. When I spoke about my children she seemed confused, and I realized that she was not sure who I was. "Why does Lucy dress me up?" she said. Lucy was her maid who had been with her for years. "Why does she make me sit here when there is nothing to do and no one to see?"

As I looked at her, still dignified and resolute, I remembered her unhesitating courage when she had taken Oscar Wilde's two sons into her house and shielded them from the scandal that surrounded the man who had been her dearest friend. She had been a woman of note then, the friend of Henry James, H. G. Wells, and Elgar. Now there was nobody; and she was just a lonely woman, living in a small flat, and already separated from life. There was something regal and tragic in her isolation.

The last thing she said to me in a lucid moment was, "Give my love to my little Vinnie", seeing him still no doubt as a baby in her arms. As I closed the door her eyes were full of tears. I called down the stairs to Lucy, who said to me, "She will not live another week." Before I reached Los Angeles she was dead.

When I arrived at the Beverly Hills Hotel I found an enormous script on my dressing table (I have it still), called "The White Rajah" by Errol Flynn. In a covering letter I was told that it was merely a first draft, and was invited to criticize it freely.

I criticized it freely all right. I positively lashed into it. Flynn had turned my synopsis into a ridiculous story about a girl who dressed up as a boy and followed James Brooke through the jungles of Sarawak. But apart from the triteness of it, it was full of inaccuracies, not the least of which was to make out that James Brooke was a Casanova. Errol Flynn might be, but not the First White Rajah of Sarawak. He had been shot in battle when the Burmese invaded Assam in 1824, and the wound had for ever stilled his sexual passions and left him a confirmed bachelor.

The thing was an absurdity, and I wrote and told Warner Bros. so. They must have passed my letter on to Errol Flynn, because a few days later I had a letter from him, asking me to dinner.

This was an evening I shall never forget. When I arrived at his house, I was ushered into a large sitting-room with leopard rugs on the floor and furnished in the glossiest style. It was so dimly lit that the servant had to lead me to an arm chair; in a subdued whisper, he told me that Mr Flynn would be down in a moment. I waited; and suddenly, the staircase became brilliantly floodlit. On it there appeared Errol Flynn himself in a pair of white close-fitting trousers that showed every nerve and muscle of his body. Slowly and gracefully he descended, giving me plenty of time to appreciate his entrance – and him. He flashed a smile at me that would have sent a thousand fans into hysterics and then he started to make me a drink. The lights slowly dimmed, and I could only just see him across the room. We had no time for conversation before the lights blazed on again, to herald the arrival of Lillie Damita. She also wore white; a gorgeous creature, holding an enormous Persian cat in her arms. She greeted me briefly, and proceeded to lie on the floor and play with the cat. It was the most sensual and feline exhibition I have ever seen.

After these preliminaries, we went in to dinner; and I at last had a chance to ask him why on earth he had written such a fantastic story round James Brooke. He did not seem to like that, and half-rose from his chair to leave the room; but Lillie Damita laid her hand on his arm and he sank back again. He said that he had always imagined that the First White Rajah was like him – and I agreed that he was perfect for the part. I then asked him if he was aware of the fact that James Brooke had been severely wounded in India, and deprived of his manhood. That he had once become engaged to a girl who had thrown him over when he told her that they could never have any children. By this time, Flynn was frowning furiously.

"Another thing," I said; "James Brooke was the first white man ever to set foot in Sarawak. Do you think for one moment that the primitive and savage Dyaks would have allowed an English girl to follow him through the jungle? They would have taken her head and smoked it, and there would have been an end of your story."

He took my criticism with a laugh and a shrug of his shoulders. "You cannot have a motion picture without love," he said.

"And you cannot have James Brooke with it," I replied. We parted good friends; but although I stayed on in Hollywood for a month, I never caught a glimpse of the Warner brothers. Eventually I returned to England, sadder and wiser than when I left. There was some further correspondence, but no film; I suppose my synopsis lies buried somewhere in the "Abandoned Scripts Department" at Warner Bros.

I travelled widely in those years immediately before the Second World War, often combining some new place with my regular voyages to and from Sarawak. In this way I visited Australia, China, Hawaii, and Japan. I remember comparatively little of these trips, and that hardly worth recording; parties in Honolulu with a delightful girl called Freddy Mann; a curious, rather tense stay in Tokyo. All that remains in my memory is a fragmentary montage of people, places, events, too vague to merit description.

Back in England, Vyner bought a house at Bracknell, which, at last, seemed to be the answer to all his restlessness. Here he threw himself into creating a show garden; and he won several prizes for his rare specimens of chrysanthemums and gladioli. His current girl friend was the one who had arrived on the doorstep selling flags for charity; and she worked on it with him. Of all his girl friends she was the one I liked the best; she had been married, and there was little doubt she knew how to handle men.

Vyner and I had given up sharing the same room, or even the same house, and I had a flat near Knightsbridge. Our sex life was over, and after twenty-four years of marriage we had settled into a state of perfect friendship that held us close until the end. Strange to say, Vyner, with all his desire for adventures with women, was not what I would call a great lover, nor even, as the saying goes, "good in bed". He made love just as he played golf – in a nervous unimaginative flurry.

Then quite suddenly the Earl of Inchcape died of heart trouble, leaving Noni a widow with four step-children, and a son and daughter of her own. They were all devoted to her, and she has never failed them.

It was at this time in our married life that Vyner developed a mania for practical jokes. I remember, one night when he had come up to London to stay in the spare room that I always had ready for him, I suddenly woke up and found a man with flaming red hair and a flaming red beard lying beside me. For a moment I was too petrified to move. Then just as I was about to scream I caught sight of the famous Brooke nose. The next morning I said to him. "If by some miracle I have another baby and it has red hair, I will know the reason why."

On the day that war was declared I was on board the *Queen Mary* on my way to fulfil a lecture tour in the United States. That night the ship showed no lights, for fear of submarines, and we crept about the dark decks, quite numb with the sense of disaster – a disaster my father had predicted would occur ten years after the Treaty of Versailles.

When we reached New York the lights went up again, and we seemed to have left most of our despondency behind us. America at that time was uninvolved; this was not *their* war; it only concerned Britain and France – anyway it would soon be over.

My lecture tour was strenuous and exhausting, involving interminable travelling by train, then changing into my royal Malay sarongs, holding press conferences, interviews, and often private parties. Then more trains and yet more, from one end of the United States to the other. In the middle of it all I was told that my mother had died. What was I going to do about it? What could I do, when I was under contract? The show had to go on! The Press asked me if I would like the news suppressed until after my lecture that day – a very considerate gesture and one I fully appreciated.

And so, as "The Queen of the Head-Hunters", I threaded my way from State to State. It was a wonderful experience; but at times I felt that I could not go on, and only the cordiality and sympathy of my audiences made it bearable; they really seemed to want to know about Sarawak. They would ask innumerable questions, the commonest one being, "Why the heck did you marry a nigger?" When I told them my husband was English they were quite baffled; how could he be English *and* a Rajah? Then I had to tell them the story of James Brooke and all that followed after.

I had only two more cities to visit – two more train journeys, press conferences and so on, but by this time I was suffering from shattered nerves and loss of voice. The very thought of appearing on a platform reduced me to floods of tears. I returned to New York with the tour unfinished to find an infuriated manager, who swept me out of his office with my payment cut by half for breaking my contract. I suppose he was within his rights; I had let him down; but it meant that I was stranded in New York with very little money, and very poor prospects of getting any. At the outbreak of war, Vyner had sailed immediately for Sarawak, but when I cabled him, the only reply I received was that my husband had left and his destination was unknown.

There followed one of the most bizarre and miserable periods in my life. Vyner had vanished; the British Ambassador – whom I had known as an extremely tiresome small boy and to whom I applied for help – professed himself unable to do anything; I tried for numerous jobs, and failed to get any of them; and was finally reduced to telling fortunes at Leon and Eddy's Bar, where I was known as "Toots". Meanwhile, I lived on hot dogs in my room, and crept in and out under the increasingly hostile eyes of the manager.

My salvation came at last in the form of a commission to write a 3000-word article about Sarawak for a magazine, for which I was paid a wonderfully, ridiculously large sum of money. Imagine my relief when I held that cheque in my hands! I could repay my debts, and face the hotel manager once again.

I finally received a cable from my husband to say that he was now back in Sarawak and would I join him there. Would I! With the rest of the money from my magazine article I paid my fare and was on my way.

22 *A Rajah's problems*

IN Sarawak, Gerard MacBryan, whom Vyner had considered "wonderful, but nuts" at that meeting I described earlier, had settled down and done brilliantly. He had mastered the Malay language, and this had been of great assistance to Vyner in negotiations for a historic peace-making between the Dyaks and Kayans at Kapit Fort in 1924. He had an amazing capacity for getting into the minds of these primitive people which deeply impressed my husband. Whatever reservations he might have had about his character, he found him increasingly useful.

Personally, I distrusted him. He seemed to me both ambitious and unscrupulous, and I had a shrewd idea that, by making himself indispensable, he hoped that Vyner might nominate him as his successor. It was all too possible. We had no son, and Vyner was nothing if not unpredictable. A whim might become a fact, a fact a command, and a command a Proclamation. There was nothing to stop him, any more than there had been anything to stop James Brooke taking the succession from one of his nephews and giving it to the other.

This might have been fine if Gerard MacBryan had been less unstable. Those early rumours of his persecution mania at Lundu were mere straws in the wind; they were the black side of an extraordinary, almost megalomaniac imagination, which had begun to visualize a Moslem Empire stretching from Morocco to the Philippines, with himself as its leader, ruling from Sarawak. To show that this was more than political theorizing, he was converted to Islam, married a Malay girl, according to Moslem rites, in Singapore, and had gone with her on a pilgrimage to Mecca. Nearer home, he attempted to enlist my sympathy; and when I wouldn't have anything to do with his wild schemes, he tried his blandishments on Noni – but she merely laughed at him. And, all the time, Vyner continued to trust and rely on him, and I hadn't the heart to disillusion him.

At the outbreak of war, MacBryan had been of military age, and his British passport had been endorsed with an order that he should report back to England for active service. But, somehow, he had "lost" his British passport, on a trip between Singapore and Sarawak; and a Sarawak passport had been issued to him in its place. This suited his book very well, because it enabled him to induce my husband to exempt him from joining up, on the pretext that he was now not only the Rajah's private secretary but also a Member of the Supreme Council.

The odd, and, to me, tragic thing was that Vyner, in a way, saw through him. He knew the man was dangerously unstable, but for some reason he was under the spell of his charm and the force of his personality. He had seen the symptoms of insanity, the nervous breakdowns; he had even sent him away at times; but he had always taken him back again. He nicknamed him "the Baron" after Baron von Munchausen, the German cavalry officer who had been renowned for his fantastic and irresponsible yarns, and the title clung to him.

Very soon after I arrived in Sarawak in 1939, the question of the succession was solved, to all appearances, by the appointment of Anthony Brooke (also known as Peter) my brother-in-law's only son, as Rajah Muda. The title did not legally constitute him as heir apparent, but it did imply that he might succeed to the Raj; and when Vyner made a short expedition into the interior he sent for Anthony to come to Kuching to act as Deputy.

This did not fit in with the Baron's plans at all; and I have always believed that he deliberately set about the job of making young Anthony destroy himself. This is hypothetical; what is certain is that Anthony's appointment was a direct menace to his own position; and as soon as Vyner left Kuching, the trouble began.

Anthony Brooke had none of the shyness and simplicity of his uncle. Even in his earliest years he was an exhibitionist. Now, as Deputy and Rajah Muda, he was eager to show that he had very definite views about Sarawak and its administration. Possibly under the Baron's influence, he began to display symptoms of *folie de grandeur*. He had a golden cardboard crown clamped on to his car, and issued instructions that all ox-carts, motor cars, and rickshaws were to draw to one side at his approach: more serious, he started to criticize the running of the Sarawak Service itself, and canvass for its reform.

Knowing Vyner's impatience and anger at any interference, I waited trembling; but, for a time, he held his hand, either out of affection for his brother or because of Anthony's extreme youth. He returned from his jungle tour; and when, shortly afterwards, we left for England, the irresponsible young Rajah Muda remained in command.

This was by no means a popular move, and no sooner had we returned to England than four of our senior officers resigned; and the Chief Justice and the Chief Secretary wrote and told us they were considering retiring. Rumours of disquiet amongst the Malay Datus kept pouring in on us. Personally, I was convinced that the "Baron" was behind the unrest. I could well imagine him chuckling and cracking his knuckles – a habit he had – as he organized his campaign against Anthony Brooke.

At all events, Vyner's patience suddenly snapped, and Anthony Brooke received notice from him that a Proclamation had been issued in Kuching depriving him of the title and rank of Rajah Muda. So, once more, the question of the succession lay open; but, as it happened, it was a question that never required an answer. Not far over the horizon, infinitely more drastic and disastrous changes than any in Sarawak's troubled history were waiting, poised, to strike.

23 *War engulfs Sarawak*

THE YEAR 1941 marked the centenary of Brooke rule in Sarawak; and Vyner announced in March that, to commemorate it, he was proposing to surrender his absolute powers and introduce a written constitution with a democratic, representative Legislative Council.

In his formal address at the Court House to the President and Members of the Supreme Council and the Committee of Administration, he said:

"... When this Constitution is promulgated I will thereafter legislate by and with the advice of the representative Legislation.

By voluntarily surrendering these great powers I feel that I shall be making a contribution towards the interests and welfare of the people commensurate with the spirit in which the first Rajah received the Government of this country and the auspiciousness of this Centenary.

I wish to say that for a long time I have felt the need and desirability of ending the period of Autocratic Rule in Sarawak and substituting for it a Liberal Constitution. But now only do I feel that the time is ripe for effecting this great change in the traditional method of Government in Sarawak.

I have always been positive, as was my father, that it was

never the intention of Sir James Brooke to establish a line of absolute rulers. What he set out to do was to protect the natives of Sarawak until such time as they could govern themselves...."

In his reply to Vyner's announcement, the Chairman of the Committee of Administration thanked the Rajah profoundly for the proposed reforms, and went on:

"... We solemnly declare to Your Highness that Your people will always look back with heartfelt gratitude to the years of Absolute Rule by the three Rajahs which has led them to the day on which Your Highness is able to feel assured that a measure of Democratic Freedom may be extended to them and yet all will remain well in Sarawak."

Personally, I think this Proclamation was ill-timed; though many people, especially in Britain, felt that a new Constitution was needed and that one-man rule was an anachronism. The Absolute Rule of the Rajahs had turned Sarawak from a country of savagery and barbarism into one of prosperity – amply demonstrated by the gift of one-and-a-half million dollars to Great Britain's war effort – a gift for which she received scant thanks, and none of the protection guaranteed by the Treaty of 1888. Any defence expenditure available went to Singapore; as Vyner himself noticed, not without bitterness.

No-one in Sarawak had the slightest premonition, of course, that the country was about to be invaded by the Japanese, in spite of the fact that they were strengthening their position on the mainland of South-East Asia. And so, war or no war, we continued our Centenary Celebrations with speeches and performances, horse races, and triumphal arches throughout the town. At night we lit up Kuching in a blaze of fireworks, and the river was thronged with decorated boats. Little did we know that the Japanese attack was only three months away.

Vyner's Proclamation had been received with apathy or doubt by the various tribes. They were still too simple to grasp what it entailed. He had said that they would be self-governing; yet he still held the reins in his hands. Though there were to be native representatives on the Council Negri, it was he, my husband, who would still nominate them. The Autocracy was still there, and yet not there. What did it really mean? That was the question on everyone's lips. What would happen now that Vyner was no longer an autocratic ruler but a Constitutional Monarch?

Many have written that the last White Rajah was a tired man. Admittedly he was nearing seventy; but I know it was only after months of consideration as to what would be best for his people that he reached his decision. All the same, I could not help seeing MacBryan's work in it; for, to me, Vyner was agreeing to become what he had always sworn he never would – a puppet king. The attitude of the people and the Government officials to the new Constitution was not so much adverse as abashed. They felt, as it were, deserted and let down, as if, in freeing Sarawak from autocracy, Vyner had thrown his country to the wolves. He tried to explain to them that his autocratic rule had become a barrier holding back their progress; and that by giving up some of his powers, he was giving them control of their own destiny. "All I have set out to do," he said, "is to protect you. You, who are the real owners of this land, will now be free to save yourselves from exploitation and oppression until such time as you can govern yourselves and become an independent State." Yet the feeling of insecurity persisted.

After the Centenary, Vyner presented me, the Baron, several of the Malay and Chinese dignitaries, and his Government officers, with various grades of the Order of the Star of Sarawak. Mine was the highest, and the citation read as follows:

To our beloved Consort, Sylvia Leonora Brooke, Ranee of Sarawak – Whereas we, Charles Vyner Brooke, Rajah of Sarawak, Sovereign of the Most Excellent Order of the Star of Sarawak, being desirous of conferring upon you, Sylvia Leonora Brooke, a token of our recognition, now therefore we do hereby appoint you, the said Sylvia Leonora Brooke, to be a Grand Master of Honour of the Most Excellent Order of the

Star of Sarawak with all the privileges and rights pertaining thereto. And we do gladly admit you to be Grand Master of the said Most Excellent Order, the honour and dignity of which we are assured that you on your part will worthily uphold.

C. V. Brooke
Rajah of Sarawak

Given at the Astana under our hand and seal this first day of September, in the year of Our Lord one thousand nine hundred and forty-one, in the twenty-fourth year of our Reign.

The ceremony took place in the garden just below the Astana steps. As Vyner put the red, yellow, and black ribbon with its magnificent golden star across my shoulders, his hands were trembling. He was nervous on this occasion even of me; and I could almost feel him thinking to himself, "She's got her father's brain. I'd better be careful of her!"

While the "Baron" was receiving his, I remember turning to one of our Senior Residents, Mr Swayne, and saying, "I would rather see a rope round his neck, wouldn't you?" The reply of our dear Resident, who had been deprived of becoming Chief Secretary by him, was hardly suitable for this book!

It was not long after this that Vyner began to have fears for my safety, for the clouds of war were beginning to throw their shadow over the Far East. I wanted to stay in Sarawak with him; but he, aided and abetted by the "Baron", who was only too eager to see the last of me, insisted on my returning to England. And so, reluctantly, I left for home; while Vyner, accompanied by the "Baron", went to Australia. There was only time for one meeting of the new Council Negri when the news came of the sudden attack by the Japanese on Pearl Harbour.

How quickly war, when it came, washed over the Far East. Great Britain's contribution to her small Protectorate was a garrison of the 2nd/15th Punjabis Regiment who knew nothing of the jungle. Twelve days after Pearl Harbour, an invasion force of about ten thousand Japanese arrived off our oilfields at Miri, the installations of which had been previously destroyed; and on Christmas Day Kuching was in their hands.

I think we had all realized that the Second World War might eventually spread throughout the Far East; but no-one anticipated a disaster on the scale of that which now engulfed us. The amiable and optimistic Governor of Singapore had assured Vyner that the city was impregnable; and it was on the basis of that conviction that he left Sarawak and went to Australia with a relatively easy mind.

The fall of Singapore and the invasion that followed were, I think, the most bitter moments in my husband's life. He was completely shattered by the Japanese occupation of Kuching, which took place while he was away on what his people might presume was a "spree", and his brother, and his nephew whom he himself had but lately dismissed from the Service, were also out of the country. He felt like a deserter. He succeeded in flying back as far as Batavia, but no-one would take him on from there. In vain he pleaded that, if he could be amongst his people, he could organize the Dyaks, and raise some sort of defence, and that his mere presence in Sarawak would put heart into his Government officers and everyone throughout the country. "What do you think, Mip?" he wrote in a letter I received months later, "They told me I was too old to be a guerilla leader. I am furious and fed up and thoroughly disgusted and I intend to remain in Batavia on the chance that they will change their minds."

But they never did. He waited and waited until, at last, he gave up hope and returned to Australia. The whole of the Archipelago had by then fallen into the enemy's hands; and I again lost all contact with him. Letters were censored, lost, or destroyed, and the dark curtain of war was drawn down over our beloved country.

"I blame myself," Vyner kept on repeating when he finally rejoined me, "but the heaviest burden of all lies upon the shoulders of the Governor of Singapore. I blame the British Government for their inadequate protection; and I blame God for not answering my prayers. Sarawak was being plundered and I was not there.

I have failed my country, and lost some of my oldest and best friends."

But if he had been there, the Japanese would have undoubtedly captured and killed him. They wanted him above all men as their show prisoner. So, although it broke him up, not being with his people when disaster struck them, I had something to be thankful for. At least his life was spared.

24 *The cloud over the future*

================

ACK in England, the bombing of London continued, and the war news was of one disaster after
another. I took a flat in Albion Gate and looked
around for something useful which I could do. Noni had been
driving a Red Cross ambulance throughout the "blitz", and was
now immersed in the "Bundles for Britain" campaign, standing
in a confusion of other people's clothes from early morning until
late at night, sorting and wrapping and tying up parcels. Didi and
Vava were working in a military canteen. I tried to join some
group, but nobody seemed to think there was anything I could
do; it seemed I was too late.

In 1943 Vava married Pepi, a huge man with the face of a medi-
tative goat, who had a big business importing oranges from Spain.
I could see nothing alluring in him myself; but perhaps, for her,
his very size was symbolic of security and peace; or perhaps those
sleepy, introspective eyes smoothed over the dust and devastation
of war. Whatever it was, she fell desperately in love with him,
married him, retired from the canteen and went into the country.

They lived at Maidenhead in a house with a tree growing
through the middle of it. Time had taught me not to be astonished
at anything connected with any of my three daughters, so I accepted the tree bulging through their roof as the most natural
thing in the world; and when I found that Pepi Cobarro was

growing mushrooms in one of the spare closets, that seemed quite natural, too. After all, in this topsy-turvey world and topsy-turvey marriage, what were a few mushrooms in an empty closet – as long as you did not mind the smell of manure. But I could sense that things weren't going too well between them, and found myself wondering who, and what, the next husband would be.

I worried a great deal about what was going to happen in Sarawak once the war was over. Vyner was out of my reach, in Australia with Gerard MacBryan – and I did not trust MacBryan. I knew his hold over my husband, and I knew that the one flaw in Vyner's character was a too great readiness to listen to others at the expense of his own judgment and sound sense. It was all one with his simplicity, his shyness, and his modesty. He sometimes felt other people knew better than he did – and this was particularly the case with MacBryan. Moreover, after the fearful blow of being away from Sarawak when the invasion took place, he would be at an even greater disadvantage.

I had no means of knowing what line MacBryan would take; but it would, I was sure, be of a kind that would tend towards the advantage of one person only – himself. I used to torment myself with thoughts of him working on Vyner to persuade him to retire, and nominate him as his successor; and events at about that time lent colour to my suspicions. It was during this period, I am convinced, that the situation, the mood, that led to the cession immediately after the war, was created – and created by MacBryan.

It was not merely that Vyner had never been able to face opposition, preferring always to take the line of least resistance; but he had a perfectly sound precedent, if he wanted one. Had not James Brooke, the first White Rajah of Sarawak, hoped that one day Great Britain would take over and accept his State? Had he not written in an old, battered diary: "I once had a day-dream of advancing the Malayan race by enforcing order and establishing self-government amongst them"? As early as 1843, James Brooke had offered to give Sarawak to the British Crown; Charles Vyner Brooke would only be reverting to his great-uncle's plan. . . .

Anyway, there were other problems nearer home, in which I

thought I detected the malign influence of MacBryan. For Anthony Brooke had again been forgiven, and been reinstated as the Rajah Muda. He was at that time the head of a provisional Government set up in London to administer Sarawak affairs – a kind of government in exile – and empowered to negotiate with the Colonial Office on Vyner's behalf. But Vyner was still the Ruler of the country, and it was Anthony Brooke's duty, as head of this provisional Government, to obey the Rajah, whatever his inner feelings may have been. But when he heard rumours that his uncle was contemplating ceding to the Crown the country which he himself now hoped and believed he would inherit, it was natural enough that he should resent and oppose it. In his dealings with the Colonial Office he did all he could to be obstructive and unco-operative, and on 12 October 1945 he received the following letter from my husband:

Dear Sir,

Thank you for your letter dated October 8th enclosing Counsel's opinion. I have now studied the files regarding the political negotiations between His Majesty's Government and my delegates, and I am deeply shocked that you should have adopted such an intransigent attitude in diplomatic negotiations.

The proposals made by His Majesty's Government were eminently reasonable, having regard to the War and that Sarawak was overrun; and I am not surprised that the Secretary of State for the Colonies should have written to me personally, complaining that "The Sarawak Representatives have so far shown themselves unresponsive to the proposals of His Majesty's Government" and that "You will share my concern at this long delay". And I have no doubt that the repercussions consequent upon the attitude of my delegates will be grave and far-reaching.

My disappointment at your conduct of these political negotiations is emphasised by your personal conduct which caused you to expend no less than twenty thousand pounds of Government money on a residence for yourself and five thousand pounds as an allotment for furniture and fittings. And I have decided to inform you that you may neither use in future the style and title of Rajah Muda nor consider you have any right of succession to the Raj of Sarawak; while I have today communicated this decision to the Secretary of State, for the formal cognisance of His Majesty's Government. I have instructed the Government agent to insert in the Gazette the simple announcement that you cease to be Rajah Muda of Sarawak with effect from 12th October 1945.

Yours faithfully,

C. V. Brooke
Rajah of Sarawak.

And so, for the second and last time, Anthony Brooke was dismissed, and deprived of his title. I could well imagine the "Baron" cracking his knuckles and congratulating himself that this troublesome member of the Brooke family had been finally removed from the path of his ambitions.

When, at last, Vyner returned to England – with MacBryan still in attendance – the Colonial Office questioned him closely as to what he would do when the war with Japan was over, and Sarawak recaptured; and how he would ever raise sufficient funds to set the country on its feet again.

There was no need to point out how greatly Sarawak had suffered and how costly her rehabilitation would be: Vyner knew that both technical and financial aid would be needed from Britain. But he did not feel that any change in the status of Sarawak should be made while her people were still under Japanese domination; and, in the face of their insistence, he wrote and informed the British Government that although he was willing to cede Sarawak to the King, it would be in his own time and when he gave the word.

I think Vyner knew that his benevolent rule could not continue. Six years of war had changed the world beyond all recognition; and in the armed peace that followed, there would be no room for the kind of small, independent sovereign state under autocratic rule that Sarawak had been for a century under the Brookes. But he knew, too, that a change should not be made too hastily.

He and Vava went back to his house at Bracknell.

* * * *

Vava had now left Pepi Cobarro with his mushrooms and manure, and had no intention of returning to him. My intuition had been correct.

There was a suite of furnished rooms below my flat at Albion Gate which had hitherto remained unoccupied; but as soon as the American Army poured into the city, four officers were billeted there. One of them was Colonel Richards Vidmer. He had been a sports commentator on the New York *Herald Tribune*, and he knew his way into women's hearts as surely as into their beds. I could see my Didi's enormous eyes beginning to look like misty pools, and I knew what that expression meant. Among other things, it meant that the writing was on the wall for poor Harry Roy. Their marriage had been rooted in incompatibility from the start; it only needed one good-looking American Lothario, whose stated ambition was to take his so-called "Princess Pearl" in his arms, to send it toppling.

Another of "My Americans" was Colonel F. P. Tompkins of the regular U.S. Army, who was in charge of their apartment in Albion Gate. It was he who told the others, after he had met Noni and me for the first time, that, "The mother is O.K. but the daughter is nuts!" This snap judgment did not prevent him marrying the "nutty" daughter three years later!

In the meantime, Vyner had begun to re-interest himself in his garden at Bracknell – and in his next-door neighbour, the woman who had helped him create it. She was in many ways the best of all his girls, and he even became quite fond of her small son. Their affair lasted for many years, until she became too possessive. Vyner didn't like being taken over by anyone, not even by me; and a coldness grew up between them. Sure enough, one day when he was sitting in the bar at a small country hotel, he saw a plump and pleasing face and a plump and pleasing figure at the reception desk. Just a flash of those blue eyes of his and a responding flutter of lashes, and the roguish neighbour was out and the pretty receptionist was in!

25 *The decision to cede*

I DID NOT SEE much of the "Baron" in those days. I knew he went down to Bracknell several times, and that he and Vyner had something on their minds, but I was neither asked nor consulted. I was merely told that my husband was about to issue a new Proclamation to his people, and I had a pretty shrewd idea what the contents of that Proclamation would be.

I think it can safely be said that if there had been no Gerard MacBryan there would have been no cession of Sarawak at that time – July 1946. It was too soon; much, much too soon. The Malays, Dyaks, and Chinese were not prepared for it. They had only just emerged from forty-five months of Japanese occupation and they were still within the shadow of the experience, the internment camps, the barbed wire fences, and, lolling in my husband's royal chair in the Astana, a Japanese commander. The Royal Chair of their beloved ruler who they had believed sat side by side with God. It was now that his people needed him; but when, not long after we had gone back to them, he said to me, "I am sending the 'Baron' to England for discussions with the Colonial Office", I knew the scales had been turned and that Cession was on its way.

I don't think Vyner had any doubt in his mind that this was the right moment to advise his people to stand at last upon their own feet, that, if the Malays had any hope of survival, it was up to them and not to him. Never before had he so believed in the maxim of James Brooke: "Sarawak belongs to the Malays, Sea Dyaks, Land Dyaks, Kayans, Kenyas, Milanos, Muruts, Kadayans, Birayahs and other tribes, not to us. It is for them we labour, not ourselves." That had been the guiding principle of James the Brave, Charles the Wise and Vyner the Good, a devotion to a people and to a country that had remained unspoiled throughout the years.

But two world wars had shattered Sarawak's seclusion, and the forces of the world beyond its frontiers were waiting at its gates. With or without the "Baron", I think Vyner knew that the days of Brooke rule were over; but it was MacBryan who forced the issue, persuading Vyner to go ahead before either he, or his country, were prepared for it, and who turned what should have been a measured and dignified withdrawal into a botched and hurried abdication.

This was the moment when a man of Vyner's isolated and secluded character needed a wife with more authority and confidence than I had. Through all our married life I had given way to him, complied with his wishes, and been at his beck and call. I have always believed that a woman should be subservient to her man, and remember, according to Sarawak custom, I always had to walk four paces behind my Rajah. I had no real say in her affairs, unfortunately.

Vyner was aware that almost everyone in Sarawak, including myself, was against this premature and hurried cession. He shut himself up in his room, and, hating opposition as he did, would hardly even discuss it.

"Do you think the Malays trust me?" he asked me once.

"They love you," I replied; "You have been their father and their friend; they will obey you like children. They will do anything you tell them, even this."

"You mean the Cession?" he said.

"Yes," I replied, "I mean the Cession."

He asked me what I really thought of the "Baron", and I said that I tried never to think of him at all. But I hated myself for saying even that. He was so easily hurt; and I must often have twisted his heart by my unconcealed dislike of MacBryan, and my impatience with Vyner's utter reliance upon him.

In February 1946 Vyner issued his new Proclamation, explaining to his people that he believed that there lay before them the prospect of an era of widening enlightenment, and of stability and social progress, such as they had never seen before; and that this could only come about through Cession, which he regarded as the consummation of the hopes of his great-uncle, the first White Rajah of Sarawak.

Then came a passage that I know my husband could never, and would never, have used:

> It is constitutional that all authority derives from the Rajah. The people select the Rajah, and what the Rajah advises for the people is the will of the people. I am spokesman of the people's will. No other man than myself has the right to speak on your behalf. Not one of you will question whatever I do in his high interest. No power nor personal interest shall subvert my people's happiness and fortune. There shall be no Rajah in Sarawak after me. My people will become the subjects of the King – this is for your good – My Royal Command.

That imperious style was not Vyner's, I'm certain. I knew so well the flowery vocabulary in which he was accustomed to address his people; and I knew the fairness and honesty of his disposition. It was only five years since he had divested himself of his absolute legislative power. Would he have completely ignored the Supreme Council, the Committee of Administration that he himself had formed? Would he have violated his Oath of Accession by not consulting his brother the Tuan Muda, and disregarded his father's wishes? No. That was not Charles Vyner Brooke, third White Rajah of Sarawak, speaking; that was not Vyner, ignoring his brother and his Government officers and declaring that the Brooke dynasty had come to an end. That Proclamation was MacBryan's work; and without MacBryan, indulging his lust for power in the only way open to him – through his influence on Vyner – there would have been no Cession on 1 July 1946.

That it would have had to come sooner or later I am quite sure. The Japanese occupation had disrupted the lives of the peoples of Sarawak, and destroyed the omnipotence of the white man. The Chief Secretary had been murdered, the Government officers tortured, and Sarawak had been plundered deliberately and undisturbed. Oddly, there had been no fear or consternation at the appearance of enemy troops in Kuching; only a stupefied realization that British protection had been no defence at all. For three generations the people had felt secure under the Brooke rule, and not one of the three White Rajahs had betrayed their trust; but the war had changed all that, and the whole foundation of their country was in ruins. Could one ageing man rebuild it, refill the empty treasury, and re-assure the anxious people? I doubt it. To cede Sarawak to the King was the only ultimate solution. But this unnecessarily hurried finale to a legend that had been such a splendid thing was tragic and heartbreaking to those who had to stand by helplessly and watch it happen.

I made one last desperate effort to delay the Cession. I tried to break the Salic Law, and place Leonora on the throne; but Vyner would have none of it: and indeed, by then, he was already too deeply committed to draw back. To be fair, there were many who were in favour; but there were also many more who were against it. Vyner's argument was that the wealth of his country had been destroyed; he could not restore it except by foreign exploitation; and this he would never do. He would rather make the King of England his heir than throw Sarawak to the commercial wolves who would devour it.

And so, one day, the Secretary of State for the Colonies announced in the House of Commons the proposed Terms of Cession. I never knew them, and do not propose to weary the reader with them here. All Vyner ever told me was that we could retain our titles.

The accumulated reserve funds of Sarawak at that time

amounted to about two million seven hundred and fifty thousand pounds, one million of which was to be set aside as a Trust Fund, from which Vyner and his family and dependents would receive the income, but which would, in time revert to Sarawak. This announcement inevitably gave rise to such headlines as, "Rajah sells his country for his own profit", and, "Rajah of Sarawak loses Sarawak but gains a million pounds". It was quite untrue, of course, and Vyner denied it hotly; but, like the titles of "Princesses" which the Press had bestowed upon our daughters, it was too good a story to be quashed. There was nothing I could say that would console him; and the insinuation that he had sold his birthright for a mess of pottage rankled bitterly.

We had one more visit to make. We were to travel through the interior of Sarawak to try and explain the reason for Cession. Unlike the usual stories of indigent countries struggling for independence, our people were being forced into accepting the end of the rule of their Rajahs; and it was the Brookes themselves, and the peoples of Sarawak, who would suffer the most from this hurried and clumsy abdication. For the last time I begged Vyner to reconsider his decision, to wait even for another year; but he said impatiently, "No, no, no!" and I knew how useless it was to argue.

I asked him if I could see the Terms of Cession. "The 'Baron' has taken care of everything," he said.

"I am sure he has," I replied bitterly, "especially himself."

Sadly and silently we packed for our last journey to the land we loved so much.

26 Farewell to the Dyaks

W<small>E ARRIVED</small> in Sarawak by flying-boat, landed at the mouth of the river, and transferred to our yacht *Maimuna*, which was waiting for us. Never before had we received such a tremendous welcome: hundreds of little boats lined the river banks, and behind the boats the crowds were so dense they looked like a forest of dazzling flowers with their golden sarongs and little coloured coats. No one shouted abuse at us or raised a dissenting voice; they only waved their handkerchiefs and tiny flags. When we reached the steps of the Astana we thought we would never be able to break through the multitude pressing towards us. The people went mad as they hugged and patted my husband; some of them had tears streaming down their cheeks. As I walked in my customary place four paces behind his royal yellow umbrella I thought to myself, "This is the real Rajah – this seventy-two-year-old man with his snow white hair and simple dignity, beloved and respected."

As we moved among the people, the Malay women who knew Vyner so well were teasing him and poking him with their fingers, saying, "*Tuan Rajah sudah gemok*" (The Rajah has got fat). They giggled and tittered and touched him and their little bracelets jingled in his ears; they pounded me, too, asking me why I wasn't with child. I didn't remind them that I was now sixty-two.

As the twenty-one guns thundered from the Fort we entered

the Astana, the home we had felt we might never see again. In the hallway, the Malay Datus were assembled; and one of the eldest presented Vyner with a sword that had belonged to his ancestors who had once upon a time been the rulers of Sarawak. Then, from our own veranda upstairs, we looked down upon the throng, and their upturned faces were like brown leaves upon coloured stems. They were chanting, "*Salamat rumah Tuan Rajah*" (Blessings on your house, Rajah), and, "*Salamat Tuan Ranee*". I would have felt further from tears if some of them had denounced us and called down curses on our heads instead of invoking this gracious and merciful benediction, this unanimous affection. I wondered if it was crossing Vyner's mind not to go through with it.

And where was the "Baron"? He was supposed to have met us at the mouth of the river. He had sworn he would see Vyner through the difficult period of Cession. After all, it was he who had set the machinery in motion; who had coerced and bribed and corrupted the Malay Datus into signing papers they did not understand; who had assured them that it was the Rajah's wish, that he was the voice of the Rajah and therefore they must obey. And then, when he had arranged everything behind Vyner's back, he had simply vanished, leaving Vyner to face the music alone, to withstand the disapproval of his brother, and the shocked fury of his nephew Anthony Brooke.

I would have given anything to save Vyner from being hurt as this was hurting him; but there was nothing I could do for him now. It does credit to his Government officers that not one of them murmured that it served him right. For it was largely his own fault. He had put too much trust in MacBryan, and Mac-Bryan, pursuing heaven alone knows what dark dreams of power, had utterly betrayed him. One result of this was that Vyner's friendship with his brother Adeh, the Tuan Muda, the shy unobtrusive man, delicate in body but determined in mind, who had served him so loyally and well and who loved Sarawak maybe more than any of his predecessors, and who was being set aside without consultation, his country ceded without his permission or advice, was damaged and never quite repaired.

As for Vyner and me, we were divided, too; and, for the first time, I felt a door had been slammed in my face, for which I held no key. I simply could not understand his reasoning; all I could do was bewail to myself the fact that my beloved and admired Rajah had allowed himself to be stampeded by a half-crazed young man, when he should have relied on his own instincts and judgment.

On 15 April 1946, the Supreme Allied Commander, Lord Louis Mountbatten, visited Kuching and signed a document restoring civil Government and handing the administration back to Vyner. All our differences of opinion were forgiven and forgotten as I tried to steer my husband through those two petrifying days. The mere thought of having Lord Louis beneath his roof, never mind the sight of him, put Vyner in such a panic that he was literally chewing his handkerchief with nerves.

Yet no one could have been more charming, or done more to put Vyner at his ease. I was fascinated by his magnetic personality, his humour and his gaiety; but, from the strained expression of his A.D.C., I could see that there must have been times when Lord Louis was not so easy going. When he made up his mind to do anything, he did it, irrespective of whether it was feasible or not. He could change from an easy and delightful guest into a tyrant by a turn of his head; and it was easy to see where his reputation came from.

The morning he was to leave us there was a ceiling of black cloud over the sky, flashes of lightning, and the rumble of a storm. His pilot sent word that the weather was dangerous for flying, and suggested that they should wait another day. Lord Mountbatten's reply to that was, "When I say we are going, we go," – and they went.

Before he left, he drew me on one side and said, "I want you to know how I feel about the Cession of Sarawak. Not during your husband's lifetime, not until maybe many years after he is dead and the true history of Sarawak is written, will the world know what a great gesture this truly great man has made."

When I told Vyner this he looked up from his book and grinned. "Intelligent fellow," he said, and went on with his reading.

It did not take us long to observe what effects the Japanese occupation had had on Sarawak. I don't mean simply on her prosperity; that, of course had suffered dreadfully, as in any occupied country; but the people themselves. It was as if they had been subjected to some subtle corruption. They no longer greeted us with the graceful Malay salute, their fingers touching their foreheads and their hearts, but gave that stiff, typically Japanese little bow of their heads. And this was only an outward sign of more fundamental changes. It was apparent that they had been not so much in awe of the Japanese as interested and impressed, for only those who had been maltreated and half-starved seemed to bear any resentment. Yet there had been some ghastly cases of brutality. One of our most promising young Government officers, an exceptionally brilliant boy, had been taken from the prison camp, day after day, for questioning, and tortured with such unimaginable cruelty that he had locked himself in the lavatory one morning, broken a glass water bottle, and cut his throat.

The gentle and courageous Catholic nuns, who had refused to abandon their convents and their schools, had this to say about the Japanese: "They were kind to our children; they brought them little toys for Christmas, and trees with coloured candles; we could not honestly complain." And this, too, was typical of the two ill-fitting sides of the Japanese character. For, at the other extreme, they had destroyed Vyner's library, with most of his valuable diaries and books; and they had found some love-letters from one of his girls and crudely framed them round the walls. An urge to destruction, and a kind of rather sentimental creativity, seemed to go together. There were shattered houses, devastated rubber plantations, and ploughed and broken padi fields; and yet there were signs of quality and culture in the roads they had made, and the delicate little gardens. Wherever they went they had left these monuments – these miniature gardens, and these softly-surfaced roads.

Our Malays had picked up many of the tricks of their

agriculture and of their art; in a way, that was the trouble. They did not really hate the Japanese; but secretly admired the way they went about things.

We visited the concentration camp where so many of our friends had been interned. It was a gloomy ramshackle building with wire fencing round it and etched deep with all the signs of misery and despair: crooked initials carved on the wooden walls, days and months and years marked off; torn pin-up girls, a grass bracelet, a broken wrist strap. How many human hopes had died there, I wondered, and how many human fears been brutally realized.

After we had been in Kuching for about a week we set off to visit a Dyak long-house at a little fort called Kapit, deep in the interior. We travelled by launch, first to Simanggang, then to Sibu; and there, at last, at the junction of the Rejang and Balleh rivers, perched upon a smooth grass mound, we came to Kapit. Our old friend, Pengulu Koh, had assembled many warriors from over the border; Kayans and Dyaks who had paddled there in their war boats; the river was so closely packed that we could not see the water, and hundreds of them followed us to the long-house when we landed.

Each warrior had brought his family, and they were all dressed in their finest clothes. The breasts of the young girls were brown and smooth, and their knee-length sarongs glittered with silver coins. The men were in their war coats, some of scarlet cloth with lovely designs upon them, others like goat-skin capes, flung carelessly upon their naked shoulders. They had round beaded hats adorned with white and black hornbill feathers, or else their long black hair hung down their backs as far as their waists, carefully brushed and shining like the wings of birds. There must have been more than a thousand of them. All the important Chiefs were squatting round in a great circle, with space for Vyner and myself. After a great deal of chattering amongst themselves, they suddenly fell silent; and Vyner rose to his feet.

He spoke in Dyak, which I could not understand, but there was no mistaking the assurance and authority in his voice. He was

THE RANEE IN NEW YORK,
1943
THE RANEE AND THE
RAJAH IN ENGLAND

THE RANEE

THE RAJAH, AGED 79

amongst the people that he loved; and, as always in such circumstances, his shyness disappeared.

I don't think I have ever admired Vyner more than I did then, as he stood, a tall, informal figure in a khaki suit and an old white topi, addressing his warriors and their wives, explaining to them the reasons for the Cession. He did not read his speech, but told his story in their legendary language and in the only way that they could really understand; and their faces remained as fixed as bronze images, and their fierce lashless eyes never left his face.

When he sat down again on the ground beside me, there was a long silence, and I could see that he was deeply moved. Then a young Chieftain rose to his feet and began making a passionate declaration. He seemed angry, and his voice was powerful and loud. Now and again, to emphasize some phrase, he would jump in the air and slap the ground with his naked feet. At one moment, in a burst of eloquence, he waved his spear and I thought he was going to attack us. The atmosphere was as taut as wire.

But Vyner knew these people, and shared their sense of humour. He cracked a joke – I guessed that he must have made some lewd allusion to the young girls' bare brown bosoms by the way they were wriggling and giggling and covering them with their fingers, pretending to be virginal and shy – and the whole crowd roared with laughter and scrambled towards him to pat his shoulder or shake his hand. In the meantime the young Chieftain had sat down and was contentedly chewing betel nut and spitting his scarlet saliva on the ground. I asked Vyner who he was. "His name is Juga," he replied, "a good chap, brilliant, really, but a bit of a rebel. I wouldn't be surprised if he goes far." He was quite right.

I learned much about the Dyaks' customs and legends on this last journey up the Rejang; and found it utterly absorbing. Strange beliefs that one heard nothing of back in Kuching, lay hidden in the dense thickets of the jungle, the myths and magic of primitive minds. The Dyaks believed that trees had souls, and would not dare to cut one down for fear of destroying the "antu" or spirit that dwelled within it. If an old tree blew down in a gale they would set it up again, smear it with blood and decorate it with flags to appease its soul and imbue it with new life. I had often noticed myself that native fruit trees had their trunks scarred as if they had been hacked at with an axe; and this was done, Vyner told me, in order to increase their fertility by a kind of intimidation. It was supposed to bring them to a sense of parturient duty.

They had innumerable superstitions about death. When a man died by accident, it was a sign that the gods meant to exclude him from the realm of bliss which was their interpretation of Heaven, and accordingly his body was not burned, in the normal way, but was carried into the jungle and laid beneath the trees. The souls of such unfortunates passed into animals and fish and were much dreaded by the Dyaks, who abstained from eating certain kinds of meat and fish in case they should be devouring the spirits of their ancestors.

A whole web of superstitions surrounded a pregnant woman, and these affected both her and her husband. It was forbidden, for example, to cut off creepers that hung over water, lest the mother should suffer from haemorrhage after the delivery of the child; or to drive a nail into a board, lest the woman should have a difficult delivery. There were many others. It was forbidden to pour out oil in case the child should have "tuli" or inflammation of the ears; a man was not allowed to fix his parang (sword) in its shield in case the child should be born deaf; if they broke an egg, the baby would be blind; if they killed an animal, it would be deformed. They were forbidden to dye anything black in case the baby should also be born black. To bring a turtle into a room where there was a pregnant woman meant a miscarriage, and if a woman slept under a mosquito net her baby was certain to be stillborn. Thus the whole period of a woman's pregnancy was passed in the deepest anxiety; and it did not stop there.

Dyak practices connected with childbirth itself were both gruesome and painful. Instead of allowing a woman to bear her child naturally, the moment her pains began, a rope was tied about her middle, and the midwives gradually pulled it tighter and tighter; or sometimes an immense bamboo cracker was placed beneath the bed, in the hope that the explosion would blow the baby from its mother's womb. The wretched mother was not allowed to sleep, or even to lie down, for twenty-four hours after the child was born. It was hardly surprising that Dyak women quickly lost their looks and grew old before their time; it was amazing that any of them survived such rough surgery.

Being the guests of these fierce and friendly people is an unforgettable experience. As night approaches, the Dyaks make their way to their long-house, carrying their mats and blankets. The bamboo floor creaks, and the lights of the torches cast strange shadows on the trees. A young girl steps gracefully down the notched pole which is their stairway, bearing a water gourd upon her head. Below the long-house there are grunting pigs and fowls, scratching and clucking over some grains of dried-up rice. Inside, each family goes about its business as in a village, together and yet apart. The torches splash wavering light upon a cluster of smoked and blackened human heads that hang upon a rafter above the mat of honour where Vyner and I will presently squat. These heads are not altogether unsightly; the smooth skulls look like giant chestnuts bound in a basket of pale rattan. The drone of many voices is broken by the howling of pariah dogs, or by the whimper of some baby calling to be fed.

The Dyaks are never idle. There are old fish traps and deer snares to be repaired, and baskets to be made; the younger boys whip together two curved slats of wood to make sheaths for their parangs; the old men sharpen the blades, grunting and feeling the edges with their ancient thumbs; the women nurse their babies. Children are suckled until they are six or seven; there is something strange to our eyes in the sight of a small boy running up to his mother and starting to pull at her brown and hardened nipples.

Our last evening amongst them was to be a special occasion, and from one end of the long-house to the other came the throbbing of drums, heralds of a night of dancing and feasting. *Arak*, the rice spirit that glides down your throat like golden satin, leaving your head clear but robbing your legs of motion, is passed round; and so, less welcome, are eggs that have been buried for many, many moons.

The dancing that night was the most spectacular we had ever seen, as the Dyaks slapped their hands upon the monkey-hide drums which they held in their laps by a rattan loop hooked over one of their big toes. First they tap with the tips of their fingers, and then with the balls of their hands, and the primitive music seems to express the very heart and soul of the old jungle.

Suddenly, with a blood-curdling yell, the dancer leaps into the middle of the floor, balancing on one heel and revolving slowly round our circle, his arms swaying with supple grace. Slowly he crouches and poses, kneels, leaps, bends backwards until his plumed head touches the floor, with eyes half-closed. Sometimes it is a war dance, sometimes a fight between two birds. Only much later, when the *arak* or *tuak* has really taken hold, do the dances develop a crude and highly-coloured realism as in the "monkeys' love-dance", which might make even the monkeys themselves blush for shame, or in the *Ajat Timbang Anak* in which a woman is portrayed nursing and suckling her child. Above all, the Dyaks are born mimics, and love to clown the simple acts of nature. One of their favourites is the *Ajat puar Kesah*, the dance of the itchy blanket, which illustrates the detailed horrors of sleeping in a blanket full of fleas.

Thus we spent our last night in the long-house of Kapit.

Before we left the following morning, they showed us with great pride their collection of Japanese heads, all smoked and hanging in a special corner of the long-house. During his reign Vyner had practically put down head-hunting, but he had raised the embargo on it for the duration, and the Dyaks told us gleefully how they had taken advantage of this opportunity. They had sent their prettiest daughters down to a pool in the jungle to bathe; and when the Japanese had crept out to stare at them, they had simply lopped off their heads as they went by. "Taking Japanese heads very fine sport," they told us. "Very, very funny game."

And so, we took our last leave of the Dyaks. Thousands of them came down to the Fort to see us off, and they were quiet and subdued, but I don't think they believed, even then, that they would never see us again.

27 *The end of a dynasty*

WHEN WE RETURNED to Kuching we heard that there had been a vehement debate in the House of Commons, and that two M.P.s, Mr Gammans and Mr Rees Williams, were on their way to Sarawak to find out, on behalf of the British Government, whether the people were in favour of the Cession. Both these men had known Malaya and could speak the language, but their assessment could hardly be more than superficial. Vyner and I felt rather sorry for them, travelling round Sarawak in their minesweeper, so outwardly impressive, of so little real importance; but what they saw and heard was, apparently, enough to convince them that there was a substantial majority in favour.

Just before the vital meeting of the Council Negri, when the votes of the people would be heard, Vyner's brother Adeh, the Tuan Muda, arrived in Kuching to make one final plea against it. In London, Anthony Brooke had already declared that he would fight tooth and nail to prevent Sarawak becoming a Crown Colony until the people had been properly consulted under their own Constitution; and that he regarded Cession as a betrayal.

In Sarawak, Vyner looked round at his devastated country and said, "I think that my rule in Sarawak is an anachronism."

"Who," he asked me, "has given me a single constructive plan that might contribute to the welfare of the people? All they can suggest is that we should go back to the 'good old days'. You remember what they were, Mip? Good for the Residents; good for my Government officers who acted like little tin gods. But what about the people? Had they any voice? Was there any free press that was not Government-controlled, or any possible way that they could air their opinions and state their cases? Can't you see that the Brooke rule has had its day?"

I did see, I suppose. But, more emotional, all that I could think of was that in a few years the people would no longer be singing the words of the Sarawak National Anthem:

Ten thousands yet unborn
Will bless the name of Brooke

and that a dynasty would have ended. I realized the country had quite suddenly grown up, and we and its Government were living in the past; but it made me very sad. I didn't want to admit it, even to Vyner.

Above all things, Vyner was an impatient man. He gardened ferociously, played golf with headlong speed, and made love as if there was a time bomb under the bed; so it was not to be wondered at that, as soon as the idea of Cession had crystallized within him, he could hardly wait to have it done with. All through those un-happy days he never once crossed the river, but sent me instead to snoop and find out what everybody was saying and doing. What could I tell him? That he had lost prestige? That the people's confidence in him was shaken and his brother whom he honoured and respected was his bitterest opponent? What kind of comfort would that have been to my poor husband who knew already in his heart that he had made a mistake in leaving the groundwork of the Cession to a schemer like MacBryan? I did still keep trying to persuade him to give up the idea, and once I thought I had suc-ceeded. He assured me he would hold up the whole thing; but alas, the mood did not last, and anyway he had gone too far by then. It was in the hands of the people now, not in his.

When the meetings of the Council Negri too place on 16 and 17 May 1946, Vyner, I think quite rightly, refused to attend, and arranged with his Chief Secretary, Mr Archer, that I should go in his place. This was unprecedented. Never in the annals of Sarawak history had a woman been permitted to enter the Court House, even as a spectator: it was a pretty intimidating prospect.

Adeh and I had been placed side by side, with only a little space between us; and I could hardly recognize my brother-in-law in that forbidding figure sitting stiffly in his chair. I desperately wanted to say to him, "Dearest Adeh, I am as much against this thing as you are"; then I thought how disloyal that would be to the lonely man at the Astana, whom I had loved, honoured, and obeyed for so many years. I really and truly believe that the only friend he had on that unhappy day was me.

I sat there listening to the slow debate. First, the Datu Pahlawan announced that he was in favour of the Cession, when it was quite evident from his manner that he was not. A few Malays and Melanaus of the Third Division also said they supported it. Only the Datu Patinggi, and three other Malays representing their various districts, spoke seriously against it. One Sea Dyak agreed, another Dyak opposed; the only Chinese present were definitely in favour. One man who had the courage to voice a genuine opinion was the Rev. Peter Howes, a missionary, who said that he understood that everyone's rights were to be respected, but what about the Tuan Muda? Had he been consulted? Had his rights been considered?

When Adeh rose to reply, he made a magnificent and impassioned speech. It was his final appeal, and faultlessly expressed. Terribly like Vyner, in many ways: the ringing voice, the undeniable sincerity, the restrained gestures. It was quite clear to everyone there that he was not so much pleading for himself or for his son, as for the whole population. The Cession had been badly handled, he argued; they were not yet ready for such a drastic change. And what would be the after effects? He ended with these words:

"I would rather see the Brooke line come to an end than that any family difference of opinion should be the cause of quarrelling and ill-feeling amongst the people of Sarawak."

When Adeh sat down again, there was a silence more eloquent than words. After a pause, the Chief Secretary rose and made a stumbling, stuttering speech that not one of us heard or understood; and then the voting began.

There was something pitiful – and all too symbolic – in what happened next. Members had been told that those in favour of Cession were to rise to their feet and raise their right hands; those against it were to remain seated and stay quite still; but in their excitement, everyone stood up, and the Court House became a turmoil of waving arms and moving bodies, so that it became virtually impossible to decide who was for the motion and who was against it. Nevertheless, somebody finally decreed that nineteen were in favour of Cession and sixteen against. Then, right at the end, one European Member voted against, so the final figures were, Ayes 19: Noes 17, and the will of the Rajah had been accepted by just two votes.

In this way, my husband ended a monarchy as his great-uncle had founded one. As for the capital itself, the storm over Cession had blown itself out; the gales of criticism and controversy were stilled, and it had never been so quiet. No drums, no gongs, no Malay boys singing in their boats – it was just as if the little town was in mourning for the death of a dynasty.

28 Period of adjustment

W HEN WE LEFT Sarawak neither of us spoke. I cannot describe the awful finality of that departure for the last time, the sense of waste and loss: it was such a personal thing. But I swear that from the moment we boarded the plane to Singapore, Vyner began to change almost before my eyes. He had carried his years lightly and borne himself nobly right up to the end; now, all at once, the fire faded and the broad shoulders were bowed. He was leaving some of his oldest and best friends; and the faces of our Malay boys, Jumil, Jahah, Abang, Matt, had been puckered with grief as they said goodbye. What could I say to soften his anguish? Only, "You did what you thought right, my darling. No man could do more."

I have sometimes wondered, while I have been writing this book, whether I have been right to lay bare our hearts like this. But then I have thought, "Why not try to tell the almost legendary story of the rule of the Brookes in Sarawak, and let others see and feel what it was like to be sovereign rulers of one's own state. They will learn that it isn't all roses; and that to wield that kind of power, you have to suppress your own personality and become, quite literally, the servants of the state."

On 26 July 1946, the Privy Council in London ordered the

annexation of Sarawak to the British Crown, Sarawak became a Crown Colony, and our role in her affairs was over.

*   *   *   *

And now Vyner and I found ourselves suddenly shorn of our glory, and faced with the necessity of adjusting to a world in which we were no longer emperors but merely two ordinary, ageing people, two misfits, if you like, in the changing pattern of modern times. I think it was possibly easier for Vyner than for me. He was basically a simple person, and he had simply done his duty in becoming Rajah of Sarawak, being the eldest son, and having been trained for the job from an early age by his fierce old father; whereas I had merely been Lord Esher's youngest daughter, a "Society girl", brought up to be presented at Court and to get engaged and married as quickly as possible. Sarawak, for me, was like a dream come true; and when it ended, I felt utterly lost. Perhaps I had enjoyed more than I should have, seeing everyone rise to their feet as I entered a room, and the traffic drawing to one side as I went by. But that was not much consolation now.

I think it was Vyner's modesty and lack of ostentation that helped me to keep a reasonable perspective. He returned to his garden at Bracknell, his budgerigars, and his girls, and I went back to my apartment at the corner of Albion Street. Noni had now married her American Colonel; and it looked like an excellent match. His quiet and unassuming character was an ideal counterweight to that of my highly strung eldest daughter. She was so like the old Ranee, laughter and gaiety one moment, tears rushing to her eyes the next. Tommy would take all her moods with a shrug and a smile, and help himself to another Scotch and soda.

Didi, under the auspices of Richards Vidmer, had now become "Liz", and was still infatuated with him. Dick was undoubtedly a fascinating man, with a certain type of American's easy charm and assurance; but I'm afraid there wasn't much underneath that handsome appearance except hot air. The trouble was, my darling daughters were, in their own individual ways, so hopelessly susceptible.

In the meantime Vyner had settled down once more with his girls, and every now and then I would receive a frantic phone call, "Please, Mip, come down and get rid of so-and-so for me!" and I would rush to his house and play the indignant wife.

Some people may think my attitude towards my husband's indiscretions showed a lamentable weakness in my character; that my tolerance bordered on complicity. I suppose, in a way, it did; but you must remember that I knew and understood the limits of his affections, and his odd, compulsive need for feminine company. I never looked seriously upon his girls, and neither did he; "*affaire l'aise*", he called them in his excruciating French, and that was exactly what they were. They meant no more to him than, say, another man's regular visits to his local or his bookmaker: they never diminished the affection we had for one another.

I started to write again. I had an idea for a novel about two sisters, whose father was to be a portrait of my husband; but the plot refused to jell, and the dialogue dragged. It was then that I met Freddie Knott, an interesting and likeable young man whose life at that moment was as frustrated and confused as mine. He tentatively suggested that he might be able to help me; and between us we completed *The Darlingtons*. It was by no means a masterpiece, but it was well and pleasingly written. Little did I foresee then that my sensitive and fidgety young collaborator would go on to write that highly ingenious and successful thriller, *Dial M for Murder*.

And so Vyner and I settled down to our life of retirement, he still in his house at Bracknell, and I in the Bayswater Road. How strange it seemed, how pointless and monotonous, waking up in the morning with no definite purpose, no plan of activity, and with no future to look forward to, only the past to remember.

At night I still seemed to hear the Dyak gongs and the distant resonance of muffled drums; to inhale the perfume of the flowers in the little Malay girls' hair. Would I ever cease to long for that enchanted land, or to forget that I had once been part-ruler of it; or break myself of the habit of standing up whenever Vyner entered a room, of walking dutifully four paces behind him? Now that we no longer had our country, we had a feeling of isolation, of not belonging. Where was the sentry presenting arms as we went in and out? Where were our Malay boys softly and gracefully waiting on our every wish? We had been spoiled and pampered; and now we were two lonely people beginning the day without reason and living through it without anything to do.

When I went to the country to see Vyner he would talk lightly of Sarawak, and laugh at himself for ever having ruled it. "Look at me now," he once said, "fertilizing the vegetables by taking the male to the female. A bit of a come-down from being Rajah, acting as stud groom to a vegetable marrow."

In 1947 Liz married Richards Vidmer, and the following year Vava married Andrew MacNair. So now we had three new sons-in-law, two Americans and a Scotsman. I don't think Vyner even realized that there had been any change. He was not what I would call an involved father; in fact, he always maintained that his daughters' entanglements were none of his business.

As soon as he found he could no longer stoop to plant or weed, he lost interest in his garden, his flowers, and his aviary of multi-coloured budgerigars, sold up everything and moved to London. I found him a house in Albion Street, one of a row of tall ugly houses that looked exactly alike, and which he immediately took a fancy to. I couldn't think why, until I remembered his father's austerity, his mother's Ascot home with its drab and dreary décor, and his brother's habit of lying on a bare board stretched across his bath in preference to sleeping in an orthodox bed. Vyner had the same disinterest in his surroundings. He had a few Sarawak souvenirs in his drawing-room, including two splendid brass lions that stood like sentinels on either side of the fireplace. He had bought them from an Indian who had brought them to the Astana in a sack and sold them so cheaply, and in such a hurry, that we were certain he had stolen them from some temple's steps.

There was not much else, apart from a refectory table which served as his bar, some long bookcases that housed his precious library, and a tame budgerigar that flew freely about his room. He was devoted to this little bird and gave it innumerable toys;

at the same time, with his antipathy towards any display of affection, he was sometimes rough and almost cruel in his handling of it. When it became old and ill and obviously dying, he turned his face away and said to his secretary, "Put it in the water jug." He had a remarkable way of being able to close a shutter on any portion of his life that was finished, or which caused him pain; a quality I envied but did not share. He hated the idea of death, because it was something beyond his control; I resented more the tyranny of old age. I had just begun to notice the early symptoms of rheumatoid arthritis in my hands and feet; joints beginning to enlarge, and the eternal ache. There is no cure, so what can one do but grin and bear it, and keep active for as long as one can?

By this time I had moved from Albion Gate, and Vyner had bought me the long lease of a little mews house in Archery Close, off Connaught Street, which was a perfect place for me to write and paint in. Moreover, it was quite close to him; and every morning at twelve o'clock I would walk round and have drinks with him and then lunch; and every evening I would go round again at six o'clock and stay until seven-thirty or so. Sometimes his girls were there, and always his secretary.

Sally Hussy had started as a stenographer in the Sarawak Government Office in London. She was a small, delicate thing with enormous eyes, a soft voice, and a supplicating manner, all of which concealed tremendous efficiency and ambition. Whether in those early days she had dreamed of being my husband's private secretary, I do not know; but if she had, the dream came true; and at times came close to being a nightmare. For as he grew older, Vyner became an exacting and tormenting boss, and an exasperating tease. Sally would occasionally rebel; but in the end, like all of us, she succumbed to the charm that made us overlook his total indifference to other people's feelings. The truth was, I'm afraid, that he was hopelessly spoilt. I remember his Government officers used to say of him, "When the Rajah laughs and calls you a wonderful chap, you are in danger of losing your job; but when he slaps you on the back you know you've lost it."

All these idiosyncrasies might make you wonder how I could

possibly have put up with such a man for over fifty years; and the answer is that, above all, he was fun to be with. His sense of humour and his dry jokes could set an entire table in a roar; he hated to be serious; and this was why his people in Sarawak loved him. We were such opposites, he and I; he with his lightness of heart, and I with my despondency and frequent tears, we made a perfect combination. He made up for all that I had missed when I was young.

Although for many years we did not sleep together, we never once felt disunited; except, briefly, over the vexed question of Cession, and that soon passed. He knew I wanted babies, and he gave me babies, perhaps there was more mother in me than wife; and when the sexual side of our marriage came to an end we lived our separate lives, but without severing or spoiling our relationship in any way. After we had left Sarawak, we lived contentedly in our separate homes, seeing each other when we wanted to, keeping away when we were not in the mood. It was an arrangement that suited us, and might very well suit other married couples too.

29 *Death of MacBryan*

THE DARLINGTONS was published by Farrar &
Strauss in the States, and by Boardman in England.
It got excellent notices, and our hopes were high
because Freddie Knott and I felt we had made a good job of it.
But in spite of the fact that I went to New York and made several
personal appearances, we were disappointed and the book died a
slow and peaceful death.

Three years later I wrote my final novel. It was called *Headwind
House*, and was also published by my good friend Boardman. I
considered this to be one of the best books I had ever written, but
it was rather unpleasant, with unpleasant people in it, and cruelly
true of the man I had picked for my hero. I suppose I wanted to
get even with a certain incident in my past; anyway I knew I felt
better as I finished the last page.

It was while I was living in Archery Close that we heard that
Gerard MacBryan was in a mental home in London and Vyner
asked me if I would mind going to see him. All my life I have had
a terrible fear of mad people. I have still. I have been obsessed by
the certainty that one day something awful will happen to me
through a lunatic – so it was with the utmost trepidation that I
went.

He was lying quite still, staring up at the ceiling, and I could
feel the tenseness of his long lean figure. I had no idea then that

he was strapped on to his bed. I just saw the white desperate face
fighting for control. When he looked at me there seemed to be
no sight in his small grey eyes; they were like two marbles on a
flat surface. He was very thin, almost transparent, and I could
hardly distinguish his pale lips in his pale face. This was "The
Baron" no longer; merely the void body of a prodigy whose
genius had been quenched, in which there was nothing left but
blood and breath and the grey stare of those sightless eyes.

There was a man in the next bed playing cat's cradle with a
piece of knotted string, squinting and giggling like a mischievous
child. Two orderlies stood at each end of the ward, and most of
the patients seemed to be asleep. I didn't know what to say to
MacBryan; it seemed almost inhuman to rouse him from that
blank obliviousness; I felt no bitterness towards him any more:
how could I?

"Baron," I whispered, "Baron, do you know me?"

Slowly his eyes turned towards me. There was no other move-
ment except for the claw-like hands picking at the sheet. In my
limited bazaar Malay I said, "*Apa habar Baron, ada baik?*" (How
are you, Baron? Are you all right?), which was a foolish enough
question, but I was so nervous by then, and so upset by the man
playing with his bit of string, all I could think of was how to get
away.

Suddenly MacBryan caught sight of my diamond ring. He
seized my hand and dragged it off my finger. I remembered his
passionate love for precious stones; he held it up, and there was
sense in his eyes for a moment, and a fiendish glee on his face.
"Lovely – lovely – lovely" he kept repeating; and the man making
cat's cradles held up his string and said "lovely" too.

Then the "Baron" laughed that laugh of his that shook his
whole body and had once been so infectious, and the ring fell on
to the bed. I grabbed it and fled. I was out of that building and
down the stone steps into the street as fast as I could go.

Only a week later he was released, the doctors having certified
him as a perfectly normal and exceptionally brilliant man, who
was suffering from nothing more serious than exhaustion and

anaemia. For a while he continued his twilight life, in and out of institutions. The last time I went to see him – without my diamond ring – he told me he was going to marry Princess Margaret and they were very much in love. His mind had quite gone. Never once did he ask to see Vyner, or mention Sarawak.

We heard years later that he had died in Hong Kong, where he was living in a cheap Chinese hotel. He had been picked up in the middle of the street, directing the traffic; and although he had thousands of dollars in the bank, the "Baron", with his charm and his twisted dreams of power, looked like a down-and-out, filthy and in rags. I never dared ask Vyner what he thought about the downfall of his friend.

For a little while Vyner went in for owning racehorses. He had two or three, and raced them at Northolt and at Sandown Park; but they very rarely won, and the tortures of shyness he underwent at having to enter the Paddock to see his jockey mount ruined the entire racing season for him. I happened to be with him on one of these occasions, and I saw him go up in his genial way and slap a jockey heartily on the back, saying, "Now mind you go in and win for me, my boy." Which was fine, if it hadn't been someone else's jockey! That was the end of his sortie into the perils of being an owner. He sold up and retired to London. But racing remained an obsession with him and we went to almost every meeting. He had innumerable form books and would bet quite heavily at times; I believe he was still placing bets every day right up to the time he died.

My arthritis was beginning to get worse. Dr Sinclair, who had been my medical adviser from the beginning of the disease, told me quite bluntly that I would never be able to spend the winter in England again; if I did, I would become permanently crippled. This was a terrible shock to me, because Vyner himself was not at all well. His blood pressure was alarmingly high, and he was having occasional blackouts that were frightening, though not, apparently, dangerous. He was one of those people who took any sign of illness as a personal affront and scoffed at pills and diet sheets; so he went from doctor to doctor, trying to find one who would tell him there was absolutely nothing the matter with him. However, he at last saw Dr Sinclair himself, and seemed to have complete faith in everything he said and quietly agreed to his treatment.

Satisfied that he was now well on the way to recovery, I began to attend to my own problems. It seemed that not only would Vyner and I be divided by streets and houses, but by thousands of miles of ocean, and I realized there was to be no "Darby and Joan" finale for us in our old age. I should become no more than a summer visitor, saying "Hullo" and then going off again.

As it happened, Liz and Dick were living in the West Indies, and Vyner suggested I should go out and stay with them for a while. So you could say it was a combination of my second daughter and arthritis that first took me to Barbados.

Before I left, Vyner had one of his black-outs and fell down while walking alone in Hyde Park. He was only shaken, but his confidence in himself was shattered. Never again after that did he go out of his scarlet front door; never again was Albion Street to see the tall well-knit figure in the grubby felt hat and trousers that were always too short, walking briskly across the Bayswater Road. He became the face at the window, the shadow that passed to and fro. He was enclosed in the narrow ugly house with his books, his budgie, and his girls. Half the year his windows remained hermetically sealed. He had closed his shutters against the outside world.

And so it was that I went to Barbados. I went for a three-months' visit and stayed for fifteen years.

To begin with, it was a curiously empty and unhappy time; time wasted, aimlessly drifting, without real friends, sitting at bars drinking, because other people were drinking, because there was little else to do; and all in that glorious climate, in that odd but attractive island. It was almost as if there was something rotten behind the façade of tropical fecundity, or within myself.

I used to say to myself, "I am still the Ranee of Sarawak. Surely that should mean something; surely it is something to live up to." But it meant nothing there. Nobody had ever heard of the Ranee, and Brookes were two for a cent, like bananas in the markets of Bridgetown. I was just another lonely old woman, living apart from her husband, drowning her identity in night clubs. I was consumed with self-pity. I forgot Vyner's concern about my health, his anxiety for my lameness and swollen hands, and persuaded myself that he had only sent me to Barbados because there was nothing more I could do for him; because he had his girls, his secretary, and a few fond and fawning friends. I had been somebody, and now I was nobody, and I resented it.

Liz and Dick Vidmer were living in a house called Westerley, overlooking the Caribbean. I hadn't been there more than a week before I realized that this was yet another of my daughters' marriages that wasn't working out. I wrote to Vyner and said, "You know what is the matter with those two. There is love without friendship."

The trouble was that they were both spoiled in their different ways. Every winter I went to Barbados; but I never went back to Westerley. Instead, I wandered from one house to another in search of happiness, and with an oppressive sense of doom.

Then Vava came out to Barbados, and it was as if a bomb had fallen in our midst. She had left her pinched and peevish husband and her little son, unable to put up with the restricted area of her wedded world. Vava, the figure of temptation and desire, made quite a stir on the island's beaches. The phoney title of "Princess" was revived. It was something the Barbadians appreciated and understood; but it did all of us more harm than good in that unhappy time. I found myself involved in illicit love affairs, family quarrels, face-slappings and brawls – and the Brooke family were always in the wrong. It was like a madness; a touch of that same tropical fever we had succumbed to in the Far East, and then recovered from, and now fell victims to again; a dangerous restlessness of heart that led to a dangerous recklessness of behaviour.

30 Barbados: money worries and illness

AMONGST my husband's qualities, one was conspicuously lacking: he was no financial genius. He was generous to a fault, to his daughters and me, to his Government officers, and to his girls. When the Cession was signed, he had believed that the one million pounds set aside in the Trust Fund for himself, his family and dependents would bring in an ample income for the rest of our lives. But as time passed it proved less than sufficient, and he began to eat into his capital. We had never discussed money; I never have known the full financial terms of the Cession; and it was only when I read his Will and saw the pitiful sum he had left that I knew why so often in his letters he had written, "I don't want to live until I'm ninety."

It seemed to me ironical that a man who had once given a huge sum to Great Britain, and then, as if that wasn't enough, given his country to the King, who could have commanded sufficient security for the rest of our lives, should be bowed down with money worries. Part of the trouble was that money meant little else to him except to hand out to those who hadn't any. For instance, in a gesture more generous than wise he gave Liz and Vava cash settlements amounting to over forty thousand pounds each. He thought it would be better for them to have it while they were still young, and anyway he was tired of their constant pleading for assistance. There were no strings attached; it was theirs to do what they liked with, and they spent it like water. Noni, characteristically, had given up her share to her two sisters, and was not involved except as a spectator; all we could do was stand by and watch the two of them make a funeral pyre of their future. I blamed myself mostly for this. Mr Smith, the Sarawak Government Agent, had implored Vyner to put the girls' money in trust, but I overrated their financial stability; I argued that they were women and no longer children. "They will be all right," I said, "you'll see." We saw.

In no time at all they were both in the red again; and, of course, as soon as Vyner heard about it he simply sighed, shrugged his shoulders, cleared up their debts, and gave them a comfortable allowance to live on up to the time of his death. As a result, of course, he discovered – too late – that he was running short himself; and the poor old boy became obsessed with keeping detailed and methodical accounts of all his expenditure, which he would then send to me. He spent very little on himself – God knows there was never a worse dressed man! He made his bets, and he bought his books because they were important and really all that he had left in life; but his suits were off the peg, and his shoes came from a small shop in the Edgware Road. Most of it went to his family and friends, for he was always a princely figure, and jaunty in his happy-go-lucky way. His hands were always scrupulously clean, his white hair beautifully brushed. The old rascal knew he was handsome, and delighted in it.

So, week after week, I received his balance sheets, with comments on them sometimes comic but more often sad. "If we go on like this you'll all be paupers when I pass out," he wrote more than once; but I never really believed him. Only sometimes that little flutter on one's heart called fear disturbed me. Vyner still had money to spend on us and on his friends, but none to waste; and although he never actually said "no" to our constant demands, he was finding it more and more difficult to say "yes". I would return to England every two years now – the intervals had steadily been getting longer – for a few months when the weather was warm, and it was a comforting feeling that whenever I felt lost and adrift in Barbados, there was my Rajah in London, waiting to put me together again.

Meanwhile I was in constant pain; that aching suffering of arthritis with its occasional sharp spasms which tear and torment every joint and eventually culminate in an agonizing flare-up. I had a particularly severe attack while living alone in a tiny apartment at the top of the Royal Bank of Canada. Beginning with what I thought was merely a stiff neck, it steadily got worse and worse. I tried to relieve the pain by winding my right arm round the back of my head, whereupon I became completely locked. I can just remember Vava coming and moving me into her house to look after me. The rest seemed like a nightmare, of which I remember nothing until I awoke in Cave's Nursing Home.

There, during a period of two months of ceaseless pain, through the efforts of Dr Douglas Carter and my two sweet Barbadian nurses, Nurse Codrington and Nurse Sealy, whose gentleness and patience I shall never forget, and Mrs Cave's therapy, my arm was gradually pulled down from round my neck and straightened out. However, by the time I was pronounced well enough to move, Dr Carter refused to allow me to return to my little skylight flat. Vava and Liz then arranged for me to rent a room at a club called *The Breadfruit Tree*; and, once again, the whole course of my life was changed.

31 Recovery and refuge

I WAS SICK in mind as well as in body when, by chance and luck, I came to that place of healing. There is something about the young owner Frank de Buono, a compassion, a concern, which, at that time and for the next three years, was powerful enough to help me rebuild my life. So much so that even Vyner noticed and wrote to me after one of my visits to England, "You are a different person, Mip. You've been rejuvenated." But my troubles were not quite over.

I became aware of a change taking place in my vision. I had never had very good eyesight, and for some time had worn glasses for reading and painting. But this was something different and disquieting; my sight had begun to deteriorate rapidly and I had to face the fact that I was going blind.

At first I refused to tell anyone. I pictured myself crippled with arthritis crawling about Barbados like a mole. I used to go and sit at the Ocean View Hotel and measure the distance out to sea getting less and less. Every time I blinked it was as if my eyelids were filled with broken glass. At last, in a fit of despair, I went to see Dr Carter, and he immediately made an appointment for me to see an eye specialist.

Dr St. John, a brilliant and altogether delightful Barbadian, told me I had cataracts on both my eyes. No medicines, washes or ointments would cure them; the only chance was to operate at once.

To anyone faced with the same thing, I can say with absolute confidence, do not be afraid. There is no need to be. I actually enjoyed the operation, because I could just see with one eye what Dr St. John was doing with the other. The only pain was the needle of the local anaesthetic; from then on the eye was to all intents and purposes dead; and I could watch the strong brown hands delicately remove the unnatural growth as if they were peeling a grape.

After it was over I was not allowed to move my head even a fraction of an inch for many hours; and for weeks I was forbidden to stoop without keeping my head upright. For the first five days I sat in front of a window, gazing at a fabulous view which I could not see.

The months before Dr St. John could operate upon the other eye were terribly tedious. With a patch over one eye, and the other almost completely blind, I used to feel my way along the crowded street with the taxi boys who knew me shouting directions as I went. Now, with the aid of powerful lenses, my sight is better than ever it was; but those dark months gave me some inkling of what it must really be like to be totally blind.

In 1961 I went back to England for our Golden Wedding. My absentminded husband had forgotten all our previous anniversaries, but I thought he might remember this one. He had already written and told me that he had found a new girl and could hardly wait for me to meet her. "She is a little young," he explained; and I was soon to discover that this was an understatement.

From the moment I arrived, all Vyner could talk about was the new girl. What would I think of her? Would I like her? He was as nervous and anxious as a young man presenting his fiancée for the first time to her prospective parents-in-law. Our Golden Wedding never got a look in.

On the evening in question, Sally, Vyner's secretary, and I, had been ordered to be at the house punctually at six; and there we sat, one on either side of the fireplace, while he paced restlessly up and down. "The new girl", when she arrived, shook even me. She was pretty, and rather lush, and about nineteen, utterly unlike his usual specimens. I looked at Sally, who had disapproval written all over her face; I didn't dare look at Vyner because I knew I should laugh and so would he – at my stupefied expression.

She had brought him a rose, and curtseyed as she gave it to him. I felt I was watching a scene from one of those improbable historical movies and found myself waiting for the background orchestra to start playing "Tales from the Vienna Woods". Vyner placed the rose on the mantelpiece amongst the silk garters and other amorous souvenirs; and then he made one of his funny faces at me behind her back, as much as to say, "I know what you're thinking, Mip. I'm a damned old fool. I think so too, so at least we're agreed on that." What he actually said was, "Isn't she a marvellous girl. Have you ever seen anybody quite like her?" To be utterly truthful, I never had, but not in the way he meant; yet what could I say while she was still standing there with an expression of dog-like devotion on her face? My old rascal was eighty-seven, and she couldn't take her eyes off him. You have to admire a man like that.

I thought at least we would have champagne to toast our fifty years of easy-going friendship – but not a bit of it. First of all he gave me a gin and bitters and forgot the gin; then, when I asked for another, he forgot the water. At that, I gave up the idea of a romantic evening, and left him with his girl.

We laughed over it the following day, and I teased him unmercifully about his "Lolita"; but after I returned to Barbados, I looked back on it with less fun than sadness. I was glad I did not know then that I would never see him again.

And yet when a little later Frank decided to close the Club, and it looked as if, once again, I should be homeless, it was Vyner who solved the problem by asking Frank if he would look after me and be my executor and A.D.C., and Frank agreed. That's what I mean, really. When it came to the important things, Vyner never failed me – and that was what counted.

We moved from *The Breadfruit Tree* to a private house on the Sandy Lane Estate in St. James which Frank and I still share and where he took on the thankless job of taking care of an old relic from Sarawak of nearly eighty. There aren't many young men in their thirties who would even consider it.

32 *A sovereign to the end*

ONE DAY, Frank came into my room and said "I'm afraid I have some bad news for you. The Rajah passed away quite peacefully in his sleep." I couldn't believe it, I wouldn't believe it. I remember saying, "No – no – no!" and shivering with the suddenness of the shock.

Strangely enough, only a few weeks before I had had a premonition that there was something wrong with my old man, and had even written to his doctor, to receive a reassuring reply. I have no doubt that this was Vyner's doing, to save me anxiety and pain. But the news was a terrible blow.

Frank and I took the first plane to London; but I still could not believe that my beloved husband was dead. Noni, Valerie, and Sally met us at London Airport, and we went to the dilapidated old wreck of a house in Albion Street. For years he had refused to have it repaired, and it was even shabbier than I remembered it: patched and peeling walls, sagging curtains with tottering pelmets; even the staircase was breaking away from the wall and swayed as we climbed it.

This was the home of the man who was reported to have sold his country for a million pounds; the final refuge of Charles Vyner Brooke, the last White Rajah of Sarawak. It was all so desperately sad – the money worries; the shyness that had soured towards the end almost into misanthropy. This was, perhaps, the saddest thing of all. He would go to comical lengths to avoid the window-cleaner or the postman; yet if, by mischance, he did come across them, all his shyness would vanish and he would talk quite cheerfully to them, telling Sally afterwards what splendid chaps they were. This shabby prison of his last few years had been of his own making.

The drawers of his desk had been carefully tidied, but there still remained a few letters and papers that were valuable to me. When his Will was read, it turned out that he had very little capital left and I thanked God that he had died before it all went. At least he was spared that humiliation. His diaries were witness to his unfailing generosity. He had never forgotten his friends even when he had been most anxious about my future and the girls'; and the detailed balance sheets he had sent me, I realized, had been a kind of apology for the pittance that he would leave behind.

The seven days Frank and I spent in the house were haunting and relentless; I could not believe that any moment he might not be coming down the rickety stairs. I went up to his bedroom, so sparse and small, with the walnut mirror I had given him, and the silver-topped bottles on his dressing-table; the hard, narrow bed, and, a few steps down, the sleazy bathroom with its chipped tiled floor – a clear statement about one side of his character, austere and indifferent alike to comfort and to his surroundings.

Down in the sitting-room, his mementoes still decorated the mantelpiece – the crimson garter, the paper rose, and the photos of his favourite girls. His girls who, if they outstayed their welcome, were never asked again. In a way he had kept his kingdom within those crumbling walls, behind those faded curtains; they could not diminish him or change him from being the unassuming autocrat with an inborn dignity that nothing could efface. Fifty years of close companionship had never altered his shy formality with me; and yet he was the man who had made my life complete.

His body was cremated, and a Memorial Service was held for him in the Chapel of the Order of St Michael and St George at

St Paul's Cathedral on Monday, 27 May 1963, with the Right
Rev. Nigel Cornwall, former Bishop of Borneo, officiating, as-
sisted by Canon A. F. Hood, the Rev. Cecil Cochrane, and the
Rev. Philip S. Jones. It was attended by a great gathering of family
and friends and old Sarawak hands. Nephews and nieces I had not
seen for years, were there; Anthony Brooke, Zena Dare; my ex-
son-in-law, Harry Roy; and officers of the Sarawak Service who
had been our greatest friends, and who had loved their Rajah and
served him loyally and well – all come to say goodbye.

A few of his girls were there, too, and I wondered what they
were thinking now that the blinds of 13 Albion Street were drawn
for ever and the scarlet door was locked.

The address was given by Philip Jones, so moving and sincere,
it caught Vyner's qualities so beautifully and summarized the
achievements of the Brookes so fairly, I feel I must quote
from it:

"He was one of three great men; James Brooke, his great-
uncle, Charles Brooke, his father, and he himself, Charles Vyner
Brooke. They were great in different ways. They were men of
different character and they were moulded differently by the
demands of their times and purposes. But in one thing they were
alike. One thread – and it was a thread of gold – ran through
all their policies. They were concerned, all three of them, always, to serve not themselves, but their fellow men and their
subjects. I am in no doubt at all that we can see something of
both the gentleness and the strength of God in their dealings.

First, James the first Rajah, young, adventurous, and sensitive – Charles Kingsley knew what he was doing when he
dedicated *Westward Ho!* to James Brooke. The first Rajah didn't
want the Kingdom the Sultan of Brunei pressed upon him, but
when, in 1841, he accepted it, he devoted all his life and his
fortune to the service of his people; and he made his purpose
clear, he set the key-note from the beginning, when he addressed the handful of European officers he brought in to help
him, and told them: 'Sarawak belongs to the Malays, the Sea

Dyaks, the Land Dyaks and the other tribes, and not to us. It is for them we labour, and not for ourselves.'

Next, Charles Brooke, austere, even severe, yet humane. He ruled as an absolute sovereign for forty-nine years. He enlarged his country and pacified it. When he was eighty-five – in the year 1915 – he addressed his State Council, the Council Negri, for the last time. He reminded them that he had lived in Sarawak, with his people, for sixty years, for most of that time as Rajah, and he confirmed all that he and his uncle had done by the last injunction he gave his people that day – that they should never part with their land to foreigners, the land that was their inheritance and the source of their existence, and they never have.

And then, Charles Vyner Brooke, the last Rajah, whom we mourn.

He again was different. He was the most generous-hearted of men and he was by nature shy. I've heard it said in Kuching that he would sometimes, in his shyness, try to escape from State occasions and important visitors and go to his bungalow on Matang mountain. But he never tried to escape from the least of his people. He loved and understood them. He was always ready to help, to advise, and to listen. He spoke their language, and he laid it down as a firm rule that 'the Rajah and every public servant shall be freely accessible to the public', and he reminded all his public servants 'ever to remember that they are but the servants of the people . . . on whose goodwill they are entirely dependent.'

This is one of the Nine Cardinal Principles of the Rule of the Rajahs which Sir Charles Vyner Brooke embodied in the Constitution he gave to the country in 1941, at the centenary of his great-uncle's rule. Another of the Principles provides for absolute freedom of worship, and of expression in speech and writing. The whole document is a model of liberal government.

And just as Vyner Brooke never turned away from his people, so he could never escape from himself.

He remained in person, a sovereign to the end. Only a few

weeks ago he was still upright, tall, and handsome. He couldn't lose his dignity, and he never lost his sense of fun; and his voice kept its beautiful timbre to the end.

And, like his uncle and his father, he showed himself if not an orthodox, certainly a true follower of Christ. There was never any doubt that he was there, not to be ministered unto, but to minister; and his people knew this, and followed his example. Anyone who has been in Sarawak at the great festivals of the Chinese New Year and Hari Raya Puasa – the end of the fasting month – has seen human understanding, human affection between men of different races and colour, in as perfect a form as he will ever find.

This has been Sarawak's greatest gift to the world. It is partly due to the nature of the peoples themselves, but it was the three Rajahs, and not least, the last, who fostered it.

We have come to an end; the end of the Rajah's earthly life; and we are coming to the end of an era for his country.

The Federation of Malaysia is the wisest and most promising policy for these lands, so dear to many of us here – those who understand are agreed on this; but there must be many changes, and there are some troubling signs. The Rajah in his last days found these changes hard to understand and accept – we often talked about it. And so, however much we shall miss him – and we shall miss him very much indeed – we may take some comfort in knowing that, for him, the end came at the right time.

And now, all that remains is to say farewell. All differences are stilled now, and our thoughts are with those who loved him.

First of all, Her Highness the Ranee, his devoted consort for so many years; their children, grandchildren, and great-grandchildren, and all the other members of that brilliant family.

After them, all those who knew and served and loved him as Rajah and as a friend. We are a proud company, and we shall bear ourselves proudly as we wish him Godspeed. In the tongue he made his own: *Selamet jalan, Rajah, Yang dipertuan Negara* – Peace be with you on your journey, Rajah, Highness."

I don't think anyone could wish for – or deserve – a finer epitaph than that.

*   *   *   *

And that is really the end of my story. I've tried to give some idea of the fun as well as the sadness; the sense of being present at a time and in a place where history was being made as well as something of the magic of Sarawak itself. I've tried to reveal some of my own feelings, my joys and sorrows; above all, I've tried to present a true picture of my husband, with all the fascinating quirks and contradictions of his character, "warts and all", as Cromwell demanded of his own portrait.

Beside me as I write is the little silver drum which he gave me all those years ago, with the words in his own handwriting engraved upon it: *From a Friend.* I hope I've succeeded in showing that, in spite of the occasional disappointments and heartbreaks, it was the richness of that friendship that has been the most precious and invigorating feature in a long and varied life.

Living here in Barbados, writing it all down, I remember so much of it so vividly, it is hard to realize that it is already more than twenty years since we left Sarawak for the last time. I am often asked whether, if I was offered the chance, I would go back – and my answer to that is, "Yes, like a shot." For Sarawak and its last White Rajah, Charles Vyner Brooke, are inextricably intertwined in my memory. Without them, without both of them, I should never have sat down, among the bougainvillea and the poinsettia, in this last contented refuge, to write the story of my life.

THE END

"Ian Kearns writes with clarity, courage and conviction and he has written a book that deserves to be read. Though a warning, not a prediction, its central case – that the EU could collapse if not further reformed, and that such a collapse would be a disaster of enormous proportions – is all too believable."
MALCOLM RIFKIND, FOREIGN SECRETARY 1995–1997, CHAIRMAN OF THE INTELLIGENCE AND SECURITY COMMITTEE 2010–2015

"Someone once said, 'The foolish predict hoping blindly to avoid disaster, the wise warn what must be done to avert it.' Ian Kearns provides a warning. An important and necessary book which deserves to be widely read and deeply thought about."
PADDY ASHDOWN, LEADER OF THE LIBERAL DEMOCRATS 1988–1999, HIGH REPRESENTATIVE FOR BOSNIA AND HERZEGOVINA 2002–2006

"Brexiteer or Remainer, this thoughtful and provocative book is a must-read for all those who prize a stable and secure Europe. It's not a given. Ian Kearns explains why, and what European leaders need to do now to avoid potential disaster."
GENERAL SIR DAVID RICHARDS, CHIEF OF DEFENCE STAFF 2010–2013

"We live at a remarkable time in history. We are one of the first European generations in history to escape the conflicts that endlessly beleaguered the continent. We take it far too much for granted. This book warns us in readable, intelligent terms about the other side of that peaceful, prosperous coin. Ian Kearns spells out the internal and external threats to Europe's complacency and, with clarity, spells out what needs to be done to avoid disaster. Here is a timely warning we cannot afford to ignore."
RT HON. LORD ROBERTSON OF PORT ELLEN, SECRETARY GENERAL OF NATO 1999–2003, DEFENCE SECRETARY 1997–1999